GW0568945

a Pinch of Salt

a Pinch of Salt

Classic Afghan Cookery

Rahima Amini

Quartet Books

First published in Great Britain by Quartet Books Limited 1991

A member of the Namara Group
27/29 Goodge Street
London W1P 1FD

Copyright © by Rahima Amini 1991

British Library Cataloguing in Publication Data
Amini, Rahima
A pinch of salt.
1. Food. Afghan dishes
I. Title
641.59581

ISBN 0–7043–2769–4

Phototypeset by Input Typesetting Ltd, London
Printed and bound in England by
Dotesios Printers Ltd, Trowbridge, Wiltshire.

For my husband, Abdulgafur Amini

Contents

Acknowledgements

When I started this recipe book with my husband Abdulgafur at my side, the experience was thrilling. Everything appeared so natural and easy and writing each part was fun. But in the days following his untimely death the reality became very different. I soon realised that it was only his presence, skilful help and support that had made everything simple at the time. Had I not been fortunate enough to have the help and encouragement of my friends, perhaps this book would have proved far more difficult to write and would have taken years to complete. I am grateful to each and every one of them. I am greatly indebted in particular to Abdul Wakil Nabi, who contributed more to the successful completion of this book than anyone else. Abdul checked the recipes and participated at every stage. Whenever help was needed, he was always at my side. I owe him more than I can say.

Another great friend of mine who has proved to be hugely instrumental in the preparation of the final draft of *A Pinch of Salt* is Mullugeta Dory. Mullugeta has indeed been my other driving force. His enthusiasm, his optimism and, most of all, his encouragement have been matchless.

I am also indebted to another dear friend, Valerie Stockoff, who spent much of her time polishing the language of a good portion of this book. Thank you also to Mr Pearce Carter, Mrs Elizabeth Winter and Emma Sergeant.

Grateful thanks also to Mr Naisan, Mr Nabi Mizdaq, Mr Kamal Bazaidi, Mrs Ammida Assifi for the Uzbeki recipes, and to my other Afghan friends. I am delighted to say that their help and advice over the years has been invaluable to my work. Looking back, I can only say that I have been really lucky to have such wonderful friends. Thank you all.

Introduction

A Pinch of Salt is a compendium of Afghan recipes designed for the amateur cook, the restaurateur and anyone who might be interested in cooking Afghan dishes. The title of the book is taken from an ancient Afghan saying: 'Let us take a pinch of salt together.'

The book was inspired by my late husband, Abdulgafur Amini, and is the product of his imagination and effort as much as of mine. Amini's introduction is a reflection of his attitude to Afghan cooking, with its simplicity and delicious taste. Although he did not live to see the book's completion, his personality is reflected throughout its pages. His own words here speak for him.

*   *   *

'I think you will enjoy cooking Afghan dishes. They are well within the capability of any competent cook. Some of them are very simple to prepare, and yet they are deliciously different from European food and will give you a real taste of the East.

Food occupies a very important and well-loved place in Afghan culture. In Ancient Greece and Rome it was believed that the purpose of a meal was both to nourish the body and to refine the soul, and this attitude is very much part of Afghan tradition. From the earliest days the people of our land have been interested in cooking delicacies. On national days, at religious festivals and for family parties, a great variety of food was prepared in the courts of Afghan kings. Competitions, with prizes for the winning cook, were part of the festivities, and in this way the development of ever better recipes was encouraged.

Afghanistan is about the same size as France, although the population is much smaller. There are twenty-six provinces, and each region has its own characteristic cuisine. In this book we have included recipes from as many different regions as possible.

A good friend of ours, now living in England, is a poet who specialises in Afghan folklore. In Kabul, he wrote about a couple who had a small income but a great love of good food. To solve their dilemma they sold their household effects and then had a series of excellent meals which they named after the items they had sold to pay for each one. Such a tale is an amusing illustration of our devotion to traditional delicacies.

When spring comes we love to have parties and picnics. People gather together, bringing various kebabs, *boulanees*, lamb dishes, and freshwater fish straight from the river. The meal ends with Afghan tea and fruit. Fruit trees abound; almond, cherry, plum, apricot, apple, pear and peach bloom one after the other, their silvery-white, rosy-pink and ruby-red blossoms shining against the azure blue of the sky. Under the trees we enjoy the delicious food in the company of our friends, accompanied by songs, music and dancing.

In Afghanistan, by sharing a family's company and meal and 'taking a pinch of salt together', we believe that guests and friends keep their respect and affection for each other.

The preparation of this book has renewed my grief as I remember the comforts, joys and freedom we enjoyed in my homeland, but I have written it because of my love for the exquisite quality of

Afghan cooking which I want to share with you. I believe that sharing these recipes is an excellent way to bring to you a direct taste of our Afghan culture and way of life. Good food makes good friends. The exchange of ideas about national dishes can play a real part in lowering the barriers of race, language and belief and in bringing together the peoples of the world.'

*   *   *

Through its strategic location on the ancient silk and spice trail, Afghanistan has been prey to many conquerors and colonialists, ranging from Alexander the Great to Gengis Khan and from Britain to Russia. Afghanistan became a melting pot for all the customs and traditions of the East, which combined with those of the West. The ingenious adaptive capability of the Afghans meant that the fusion of the two cultures produced an altogether unique tradition. Afghan recipes have evolved from that great fusion of customs.

I feel duty bound to make sure that this vast wealth is brought to the outside world and to all migrant Afghans, because they deserve to share the legacy of their forefathers. Afghan dishes have evolved over centuries. I feel that they should not be allowed to remain hidden within the boundaries of that mountainous country and this book is intended to serve as a convenient medium to ensure the wider use of these recipes.

I arrived in England with a young family after the invasion of Afghanistan by the Russians in 1979. This helps me to appreciate the predicament which the young as well as the old are facing. As I was not an expert cook my inability to provide my family with the kind of food they had been accustomed to back home made me very sad and frustrated. Surprisingly, however, once I began to share my problem I found my Afghan friends were faring no better. In order to satisfy the family need I went about searching for information, talking over my findings with people I had known back in Afghanistan, collecting recipes here and there and cooking with those same friends. To my surprise I was able to collect enough recipes to satisfy not only my own immediate needs but much more. That initial success encouraged me to see beyond my family table and to broaden my range of recipes to include teas, sweets, bread and light snacks.

I must confess that what I have said so far does not do justice to the true nature of Afghan cuisine. Afghan cuisine is an art created by the great Afghan cooks, whose dedication to their trade has captured the taste and imagination of the gourmet. Afghan dishes will please your eyes and taste, with flashes of bright colour and delicious aromas. I hope I have done everything possible so that you too can have in your home and on your table the art of the great Afghan cooks.

Notes on the Ingredients

Herbs and spices
Nowadays, since the population of many large cities includes a number of ethnic minorities, the herbs and spices used in these recipes will be readily available. Green cardamom is used with the outer skin split. On rare occasions, black cardamom is required. Otherwise the most common spices are cumin, cinnamon, cloves, turmeric and ginger. It is essential that both the herbs and spices used should be as fresh as possible, so that they are most aromatic and effective in flavouring food. Buy the spices whole and grind them in a coffee grinder for convenience.

Pelau masala is a colourful mix of spices used in rice dishes. To make 5 tbsp, mix together the following ground spices:

2 tsp dried coriander
2 tsp green cardamom
2 tsp black pepper
2 tbsp cumin
1 tsp black cardamom
1 tsp cinnamon
½ tsp cloves

Qorma masala is made up of a blend of traditional spices for certain *qormas*. To make a large quantity for storing, mix together the following, using ½ tsp for each dish;

8 oz (200 g) ground black pepper
8 oz (200 g) cumin
4 oz (100 g) black cardamoms, crushed

1 oz (20 g) ground cloves
1 oz (20 g) ground cinnamon
1 oz (20 g) ground dried coriander
1 oz (20 g) green cardamoms (crushed)
2 oz (50 g) ground dried ginger
2 nutmegs, grated

Tandoori Masala is another mixture of spices, readily available from food-stores.

Oil
Corn or vegetable oil is always used unless otherwise stated. Ghee, or clarified butter, is an excellent fat for deep-frying because it can be heated to a very high temperature but does not soak into the food. Olive oil is rarely used.

Pasta
In Afghanistan, pasta would always be made at home, but fresh pasta is now easy to obtain from delicatessens. Fresh pasta is essential for *aush*.

Pulses
Wheat, split peas, mung beans, chickpeas, lentils, and kidney beans are very frequently used in soups and *qorma* dishes. For best results, soak dried beans and pulses in cold water overnight.

Agar strip, *mastic* and *methi seeds* (fenugreek) are all readily available in Asian foodstores.

Garlic
A very convenient way to prepare garlic for storage is the following method:

1 lb (450 g) garlic
1 tbsp salt
10 small green chillies

6 tbsp (90 ml) corn oil
Small bunch fresh coriander

Soak the garlic in warm water for 2 hours and peel. The skin will come away quite easily after soaking. Remove the stalks of the chillies and purée all the ingredients in a blender. Seal the mixture in a jar and freeze. Where a recipe requires 2 cloves of garlic, use 1 tsp of this prepared garlic.

A note on spelling
Most of the dishes have been given both an Afghan name and an English translation. The Afghan is a phonetic transcription of Dari, one of the main languages of Afghanistan. Recipes which include *Uzbeki* are from the north of the country.

Weights and Measures

These recipes have been compiled and tested using the following sets of equivalents:

1 tsp (teaspoon) – 5 ml
1 tbsp (tablespoon) – 15 ml

Conversions within the recipes are usually approximate for convenience, but tables of more accurate conversions are included here for reference:

WEIGHTS

CAPACITY

Imperial (ounces	Metric (grams)	Pints	Litres
1 oz	28 g	¼ pt	142 ml
2 oz	56 g	½ pt	285 ml
3 oz	84 g	1 pt	570 ml
4 oz (¼ lb)	112 g	2 pts	1.15 litres
6 oz	168 g	3 pts	1.70 litres
8 oz (½ lb)	225 g	4 pts	2.30 litres
10 oz	280 g		
12 oz (¾ lb)	336 g		
16 oz (1 lb)	454 g		
1½ lb	680 g		
2 lb	908 g		

Naun Bread

Naun

Naun-e-roghani Bread with oil

Naun-e-jawary Corn bread

Naun-e-paraky Chapati-style bread

Naun-e-komach Mazari bread

Naun

Bread

Serves 6   Preparation time: 1 hour 30 minutes

In Afghanistan, *naun* is the bread which is eaten daily by every household with nearly all Afghan dishes. It is served at breakfast with butter, and at other meals without butter or fat. It is an important accompaniment to soup, *qorma* and kebab dishes. The making of this bread is so simple, I bake it daily for my family.

2 lb (1 kg) chapati flour
1 pkt dried yeast
1 tbsp salt
3 tbsp (45 ml) corn or vegetable oil
2 pints (1 l) warm water
Sesame seeds, onion seeds or poppy seeds to
  garnish

Gas Mark 7/220°C/430°F

Put all ingredients in a warm bowl. Gradually adding 2 cups of water, knead well, using the remaining water to wet your hands. Knead until a soft dough is formed – about 7 minutes. Cover the dough with a clean, damp cloth and leave aside in a relatively warm place for 1 hour. Preheat oven. Knead the dough again for 2 minutes. Leave to rise once more for 10–20 minutes.

Divide dough into 6 balls and shape them into flat ovals approximately 10 inches by 7 inches. Wet the middle three fingers of one hand and make three lengthwise grooves in the dough, beginning and ending ¾ inch from the edges. The centre groove should be slightly longer than the two outer grooves.

Place the loaves on oiled baking trays. Sprinkle lightly with seeds and bake for approximately 10 minutes.

Naun-e-roghani

Bread with oil

Serves 4   Preparation time: 1 hour 30 minutes

This bread is eaten for breakfast, or at tea-time with a special green tea called *kaymak chai* (p. 261).

1 lb (450 g) wholemeal flour
1 tsp salt
¼ pint (140 ml) warm milk (temperature should
   not be higher than 37°C/98·4°F)
6 tbsp (90 ml) oil
1 pint (550 ml) tepid water
½ pkt dried yeast
Onion seeds, poppy seeds or sesame seeds to
   garnish

Gas Mark 7/220°C/430°F

Put the flour in a warm bowl. Mix the yeast, salt, milk and oil with ½ pint (280 ml) water in another bowl. Leave to rest for 3 minutes, then add to the flour. Add the water little by little, wetting your hands, and knead well until a soft dough is formed. This should take about 5 minutes.

Cover the dough with a damp cloth and leave to rise in a warm place for 1½ hours. Divide it into 3 balls and shape them into flat ovals. Place them on an oiled baking tray. Make 4 grooves in each, with fingers dipped in milk, and garnish with seeds.

Bake the loaves for 10 minutes in the preheated oven.

Naun-e-jawary

Corn bread

Serves 4   Preparation time: 30 minutes

This bread is eaten by farmers in the provinces of Afghanistan.

14 oz (400 g) cornmeal
8 oz (225 g) sugar
1 tsp ground ginger
½ tsp ground cardamom
1 egg, beaten
3 tbsp (45 ml) corn oil
¼ pint (140 ml) milk
1 tsp bicarbonate of soda

Gas Mark 7/220°C/430°F

Mix the cornmeal, sugar and spices in a bowl. Add the beaten egg and oil. Knead well.

Heat the milk until it is about to boil and add to the dough, together with the bicarbonate of soda dissolved in a little warm water.

Knead to a firm dough and divide into 4 pieces, shaping each into rounds of about 1 cm thick. Make a suitable pattern on the top with tip of a spoon.

Bake in a hot oven until light golden-brown (about 10 minutes).

Naun-e-paraky

Chapati-style bread

Makes 15 chapatis   *Preparation time: 1 hour 15 minutes*

These chapatis are traditionally baked on a *tawa*, or iron hot-plate, but a large heavy frying pan may be used instead.

1 lb (450 g) chapati flour
1 tsp salt
1 tsp oil
1 tsp dried yeast
½ pint (280 ml) tepid water

Mix all the ingredients together and knead well for 5 minutes. Set aside in a warm place for ½ hour.

Divide dough into 15 egg-sized pieces. Roll into circles 9 inches in diameter.

Heat the *tawa* or frying pan and brush with a little oil. Cook each chapati until it is a light golden-brown underneath. Turn over and cook the other side.

Naun-e-komach

Seed bread

Serves 12   Preparation time: 2 hours

Naun-e-komach is sometimes referred to as 'the bread of Taj Korghan and Mazzare Sheriff'. It is specially prepared for newly married brides to take with them to their new homes. *Naun-e-komach* is also prepared on special occasions, for example to honour a member of one's family visiting for the first time.

3½ lb (1 kg 600 g) plain flour
8 fl oz (225 ml) hot corn oil
¼ pint (140 ml) tepid water
4 eggs
1 pint (550 ml) warm milk
2 tbsp dried yeast
4 tbsp onion seeds
1½ tbsp salt

Gas Mark 6/205°C/400°F

Mix yeast and salt in ½ cup hot water.

Place flour, eggs, onion seeds and corn oil in a large bowl and mix thoroughly for at least 2 minutes.

Add the yeast and salt mixture, together with half the hot milk and mix well. Work on it for at least 5 minutes. Dip your fingers in oil to keep them moist while kneading. Knead until the dough is firm but not too soft.

Lay out a piece of cloth in a warm place and place another piece of cloth over the first one. Now mould the dough into 6 balls placing two in a row. Fold the top cloth over to cover the balls and place another 2 balls beside the first two, so making a second row. Fold the top cloth again and cover the layer completely. Place the last two balls to make two rows of three, and fold the top cloth over for the last time. In order to keep the heat in, fold the bottom piece of cloth over all six balls of dough and leave in a warm place for 1 hour to prove.

Grease the baking tray. Now flatten each ball slightly. With a spoon, knife or fork, make designs or patterns on the loaves. Transfer them to the baking tray, brush with oil and bake in the pre-heated oven for 15–20 minutes, until golden-brown.

Serve with tea at breakfast or tea-time.

Shorba Soups

Yakhni-e-morgh Chicken soup

Shorba-e-surkh kardah Fried soup

Shorba-e-chainaki Teapot soup

Shorba-e-tarkori (i) Creamed vegetable soup

Shorba-e-tarkori (ii) Vegetable soup

Shorba-e-tarkori (iii) Chicken and vegetable soup

Yakhni hubobat Pulse soup

Piaba tokhom wa zardlow Spicy soup with eggs
and apricots

Yakhni-e-morgh

Chicken soup

Serves 6   Preparation time: 45 minutes

2 lb (900 g) chicken, with skin removed
2 pints (1·1 l) water
4 oz (110 g) onions, chopped
4 oz (110 g) yellow split peas
1½ tsp salt
½ tsp ground black pepper
5 cardamom pods
Pinch turmeric powder
A few fresh coriander leaves, chopped
1 large lemon, sliced

Wash the chicken and put it in a large pan. Cover with water, bring to the boil and remove any scum.

Add chopped onions, yellow split peas, salt, pepper, cardamom and turmeric. Simmer until meat is tender (approximately 30 minutes). Remove the chicken carcass, leaving meat in the soup.

Add the chopped coriander leaves and simmer for 5 minutes.

To serve, sprinkle with pepper and sliced lemon and eat with mixed salad and bread.

Shorba-e-surkh kardah

Fried soup

Serves 4   Preparation time: 45 minutes

3 tbsp (45 ml) corn oil
¼ lb (110 g) onions, peeled and finely chopped
1 lb (450 g) lamb or chicken
½ lb (225 g) tomatoes
1 tsp salt
½ tsp pepper
¼ tsp turmeric
1 green pepper, deseeded and finely chopped
¼ lb (110 g) yellow split peas or black-eyed beans,
soaked overnight
½ lb (225 g) potatoes, peeled and quartered
1 tsp coriander, dry or fresh

Heat the oil in a large saucepan. Add the onions
and fry until light brown.

Add meat and fry until light golden-brown. Add
½ pint (280 ml) water, and simmer until the oil
starts to separate out.

Add the tomatoes, then the salt, pepper, turmeric, green pepper, split peas or black-eyed beans
and cook for 3 minutes.

Add 1½ pints (850 ml) water, bring to the boil
and simmer until meat is tender. Add the potatoes
and simmer until they are cooked.

Sprinkle with finely chopped coriander and
serve with bread and onion salad (p. 183).

Shorba-e-chainaki

Teapot soup

Serves 6   *Preparation time: 1 hour 45 minutes*

In Afghanistan, this soup is made in individual teapots and cooked in a *tandoor* (clay oven). When it is cooked, it is kept hot on a rack over slow burning charcoal at the side of the tandoor. *Shorba-e-chainaki* is a speciality of the Kandhar province.

Because tandoors are not freely available in the UK, an earthenware pot or a heavy saucepan can be used instead.

2 lb (900 g) fatty lamb, chopped into 3-inch cubes
2 medium onions, peeled and chopped finely
1½ pints (850 ml) water
1½ tsp salt
1 tsp black pepper
1 whole green chilli
¼ tsp turmeric
3 oz (85 g) yellow split peas, soaked overnight
10 cardamom pods
3 cloves garlic
A few coriander leaves for garnish

Combine all ingredients, except coriander leaves, in the earthenware pot. Bring to boiling point, cover and simmer gently for 1½ hours.

Sprinkle with finely chopped coriander leaves.

To serve, cut the *naun* into small pieces and place

in soup bowls. Pour the soup over. Chopped onion, a sprinkling of chilli powder and black pepper make a tasty garnish.

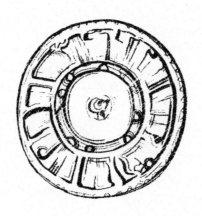

Shorba-e-tarkori (i)

Creamed vegetable soup

Serves 6   *Preparation time: 1 hour 30 minutes*

This is an Afghan version of vichyssoise.

1½ lb (700 g) leeks
2 medium onions
1 oz (25 g) butter
4 medium potatoes, peeled and diced
1 tsp salt
1 tsp black pepper
1¼ pints (700 ml) chicken stock
1½ pints (850 ml) water
5 green cardamom pods
1 egg yolk
¼ pint (140 ml) single cream
1 pint (550 ml) low-fat milk

Thoroughly wash the leeks and chop them finely.
Peel and chop the onions.

Melt the butter in a large saucepan. Add the
leeks and onions, cover and cook over low heat for
5 minutes until soft.

Add the potatoes, salt, pepper, chicken stock,
cardamoms and water. Bring to the boil, then cover
and cook over a low heat for 1 hour. Leave to cool.

Purée the soup in a food processor, or by hand.
Then return it to the saucepan and heat gently.

Beat the egg yolk separately with the cream.

Take ½ cup of purée, add the milk and mix with the egg mixture. Add to the soup and cook gently for a further 3 minutes.

Serve the soup hot.

Shorba-e-tarkori (ii)

Vegetable soup

Serves 6   Preparation time: 1 hour

8 oz (225 g) chickpeas
½ small green cabbage
3 small carrots
2 medium onions
3 medium tomatoes
1½ lb (700 g) lamb or chicken, cut into small
    pieces
5 oz (135 g) wheat grains
1 tsp salt
¼ tsp turmeric
½ tbsp grated ginger
10 green cardamom pods
2 green chillies, de-seeded (optional)
1 tsp black pepper
2 garlic cloves
2½ pints (1.5 l) water
Lemon juice and finely ground black pepper to
    garnish

Soak the chickpeas for 1 hour before cooking. Cut
the cabbage into large pieces. Peel the carrots and
onions and cut into quarters. Slice the tomatoes.

Place all ingredients in a large saucepan and
bring up to boiling point. Simmer for 45 minutes.

Purée in a food processor and return to the
saucepan. Bring back to the boil.

To serve, add a squeeze of lemon juice and a small pinch of black pepper to each plate.

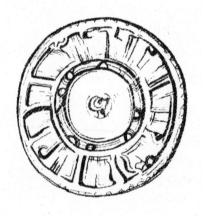

Shorba-e-tarkori (iii)

Chicken and vegetable soup

Serves 4   Preparation time: 45 minutes

2½ pints (1·5 l) water
7 oz (200 g) onion, finely chopped
¼ tsp ground turmeric
1½ tsp salt
1 green chilli, whole
4 chicken drumsticks, about 1½ lb (700 g)
2 medium carrots, chopped
2 sticks celery, chopped
7 oz (200 g) sweetcorn
3 asparagus shoots, chopped
2 oz (50 g) green beans, chopped
7 oz (200 g) fresh tomatoes, chopped
10 whole green cardamom pods
2 tbsp porridge oats
Juice of 1 lemon
one clove garlic

Bring 2 pints (1 l) water to boil in a large saucepan.

Add the onion, turmeric, salt, green chilli (whole) and chicken, cover and cook for 15 minutes.

Add the chopped carrots and all remaining ingredients (except lemon, garlic and oats). Leave on medium heat for 20 minutes.

Take out the chicken and add ½ pint (280 ml) of

hot water, the whole cardamom seeds and the oats and simmer for 5 minutes on same medium heat.

If you wish, marinate the chicken with the soy sauce, fresh lemon juice and freshly crushed garlic and grill.

Serve the soup as it stands, or liquidise to make a cream soup. The soup is best accompanied by the grilled chicken kebab and any kind of salad.

Yakhni hubobat

Pulse soup

Seves 6   Preparation time: 1 hour 30 minutes

1 lb (450 g) lamb cut into 1-inch cubes
3 oz (85 g) chickpeas
4 oz (110 g) wheat
3 oz (85 g) whole *vall* (dried beans)
3 oz (85 g) white kidney beans
3 oz (85 g) whole green peas
1 medium onion, peeled and chopped
1 tsp salt
2 fresh green peppers, de-seeded and chopped
10 cardamom pods
Piece of fresh ginger, finely chopped
¼ tsp turmeric
1½ pints (850 ml) water
2 cloves garlic
Lemon juice and freshly ground black pepper for
    garnish

Soak the chickpeas and dried beans in cold water
overnight.

Put all ingredients together in a large saucepan.
Bring to boiling point and cook for 1 hour. Leave
to cool.

Purée in a food processor, or by hand. Then
return to the pan and reheat.

Serve the soup in bowls with a squeeze of lemon
juice and a sprinkle of freshly ground black
pepper.

Piaba tokhom wa zardlow

Spicy soup with eggs and apricots

Serves 4   Preparation time: 45 minutes

½ tsp fresh ginger
½ cup of oil
6 oz (150 g) onions
1 green chilli pepper
½ tsp hot red pepper
½ tsp salt
½ lemon
8 eggs
½ tsp sugar
8 oz (225 g) dried apricots
¼ tsp turmeric
2½ pints (1·5 l) water

Heat the oil in a medium-sized saucepan. Chop the onion and fry until light golden-brown. Then add turmeric, green chilli and salt. Stir, add the water and bring to the boil.

Add the apricots, the ginger and sugar and leave to simmer for 25 minutes or until the apricots are soft (but not over-soft). Take the pan off the heat and leave it aside for 3–4 minutes.

Break the eggs one by one into a separate dish and add carefully to the mixture.

Simmer for 10 minutes, until the eggs are cooked. Finally add the lemon juice.

To serve, cut two or three slices of bread into 1-inch squares and place in a bowl. Pour the *piaba* over the bread and sprinkle with a lot of red pepper (if you like a really hot flavour).

Starters and light meals

Ashak Leek-filled pasta with meat sauce

Aush Pasta with yoghurt and meatballs

Boulanee Savoury-filled pastries

Kachee Uzbeki Pasta balls

Mantu Stuffed, steamed pasta

Maushawa Yoghurt and pulses soup

Pakaura Deep-fried dishes with potato, fish and rhubarb

Sambosa-e-Uzbeki Fried, stuffed pastries

Kofta Meatballs with tomato sauce

Kebab-e-bal morgh Chicken-wing kebabs

Ashak

Leek-filled pasta with meat sauce

Serves 8   Preparation time: 45 minutes

Ashak is one of the most delicious of the traditional Afghan dishes, served mainly on special occasions. It originates in the northern provinces of Afghanistan and uses *gandana*, an Afghan vegetable not found in Britain, but very similar to chives or leeks. Spring onions and fresh coriander are also added to give added flavour to the filling.

For the pasta
1 lb (450 g) strong wholemeal flour, white or
   brown
1 tsp salt
1 egg
1 pint (550 ml) water

Mix the flour, salt, egg and ¾ pint water to make a dough. Use ¼ pint water as necessary to wet hands in order to knead dough, making sure that it is firm but not sticky. Divide the dough into 15 balls and roll them out until they are about 2 mm thick. Using a 3-inch round pastry cutter, cut out as many pieces as possible.

For the filling
1 lb (450 g) leeks, washed thoroughly
1 bunch spring onions, peeled and washed
   thoroughly

29

1 small bunch fresh coriander
1 tsp black pepper
1 tbsp oil
1 tsp salt

Chop the leeks, onions, and coriander finely and mix together with the salt, pepper and oil to form a soft filling. Cover a tray with non-stick paper and sprinkle lightly with flour. Take a pasta circle and wet half of one side with a little water. Place 1½ tsp filling in the centre and then press the edges firmly together to seal them. Place the *ashak* on the floured tray and repeat until all the circles have been filled. If you wish, you may crimp the edges of the *ashak* with the end of a spoon.

For the sauce
1 medium onion, peeled and finely chopped
¼ pint (140 ml) corn oil
1 lb (450 g) minced beef or lamb
1 tbsp dried coriander
½ tsp salt
½ tsp ground ginger
½ tsp black pepper
1 tbsp tomato purée or two fresh tomatoes
½ pint (280 ml) water
15 oz (420 g) strained yoghurt
2 tbsp dried mint
2 cloves garlic, crushed

Gently fry the onion in the oil until light brown. Add the minced meat and fry until light brown. Add the coriander, salt, ginger, pepper and tomato purée, and then gradually add the water and cook for 10 minutes. Simmer over a low heat for a further 30 minutes.

To cook the *ashak*, bring 5 pints water to the boil

and add the *ashak*. Simmer for about 10 minutes, and then drain them carefully.

To serve, add the crushed garlic to 3 tbsps of yoghurt and spread the mixture over a flat dish. Arrange the *ashak* on top and pour over the remaining yoghurt. Finally, add the meat sauce and sprinkle with mint and freshly ground black pepper.

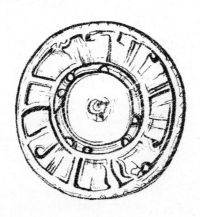

Aush

Pasta with yoghurt and meatballs

Serves 6   Preparation time: 1 hour

Aush is eaten daily by the people in Mazzare Sheriff, a province in northern Afghanistan, as a starter to their evening meal, and is made with fresh, home-made pasta. *Aush* is also eaten from time to time in the rest of the country.

For the meatballs
½ lb (225 g) onion
1 lb (450 g) minced beef or lamb
1 tsp black pepper
1 tsp salt
1½ tsp ground dried coriander *or* ⅓ bunch fresh
  coriander
1 tsp ground cumin

Peel and grate the onion and mix with the meat, pepper, salt, coriander and cumin. Knead well and form into small balls, the size of a small walnut.

For the sauce
½ lb (225g) onion
6 tbsp (90 ml) oil
1 tsp grated fresh ginger
2 green chillies, de-seeded and finely chopped
3 cloves garlic, finely chopped
5 oz (135 g) peeled tinned tomatoes
1 tsp tomato purée
½ pint (280 ml) water

Peel and finely slice the onion. Place the oil in a heavy saucepan and fry the onion until it is light brown. Add the ginger, garlic and chillies and fry for 2 minutes. Add the tomatoes and tomato purée and fry for 1 minute. Add the water and stir well. Reduce the heat, add the meatballs and cover.

When the water has evaporated and the oil separates out, cook for 5 more minutes, stirring occasionally. Both sauce and meatballs should take on a rich golden colour. Leave to one side.

To cook
8 oz (225 g) spaghetti
1 tsp salt
4 pints (2.25 l) water
3 tbsp (45 ml) oil
6 oz (150 g) cooked chickpeas
1 small carton strained yoghurt
1 tsp dried mint

Bring the water to the boil and add the salt, oil and spaghetti. Boil for 12 minutes, or until the spaghetti is soft. Drain the spaghetti well. Heat the meatballs and sauce and add. Also add the chickpeas and yoghurt.

Serve *aush* in a deep bowl. Sprinkle with dried mint to garnish, and coriander if desired.

Boulanee

Savoury-filled pastries

Serves 8   Preparation time: 45 minutes–1 hour

Boulanee may have a variety of fillings. This quantity of dough is enough for 20 *boulanee*. Each filling will make 10 *boulanee*.

1 lb (450 g) chapati flour
1½ tsp salt
1 tbsp oil
½ pint (280 ml) lukewarm water

Dissolve the salt in the water. Add the oil, mix with flour and knead well until the dough forms a soft ball. Leave aside for 10–15 minutes.

Leek filling
1 lb (450 g) leeks
½ lb (225 g) spring onions
small bunch fresh coriander
1 tsp salt
1 tsp pepper
1 tbsp oil

Wash the leeks, spring onions and coriander well. Chop finely. Add salt and pepper and moisten with oil.

Minced meat filling
1 lb (450 g) minced beef or lamb
½ lb (225 g) onions, finely chopped
1 tsp salt
1 tsp pepper
2 tbsp oil
¼ lb (110 g) rhubarb (optional)
small bunch fresh coriander

Sauté the onions in the oil. Add the meat and fry until golden-brown. Add rhubarb, coriander, pepper and salt. Cook gently for a further 15 minutes.

Potato filling
1 lb (450 g) potatoes
1½ lb (700 g) onions
1 tsp salt
1 tsp pepper
2 tbsp oil

Boil the potatoes in their skins until soft. Peel and mash the potatoes. Slice the onions. Heat the oil and sauté the onions until just soft. Add the potatoes, mix well, and add salt and pepper.

Spinach filling
1 lb (450 g) fresh spinach
small bunch fresh coriander
½ lb (225 g) leeks
2 green chillies, de-seeded
1 tsp salt
1 tbsp oil

Wash and finely chop the spinach, coriander, leeks and green chillies. Mix the salt and oil well into the vegetables.

Knead the dough and divide it into balls about half the size of tennis balls. Roll out each ball on a floured board, to make thin circles about 12 inches in diameter. Sprinkle the dough liberally with flour as you proceed.

Spread the filling evenly, but not too thickly, across half of the circle. Fold the dough in half, covering the filling, and press the edges together to seal them.

Lightly oil a heavy based frying pan. Spread 1 tbsp oil over the top of one of the *boulanee* and add 1 tbsp oil to the pan. Cook the *boulanee* over a medium flame, gently moving it in a clockwise direction until it is light brown. Turn it over, adding more oil if necessary. Continue in this way until all the *boulanee* are cooked.

Serve on their own, or with strained yoghurt or chutney.

Kachee Uzbeki

Pasta balls

Serves 8   Preparation time: 40 minutes

1 lb (450 g) chapati flour
7½ pints (4·25 l) boiling water
1 tsp salt
12 oz (340 g) low fat natural yoghurt
1 oz (25 g) melted butter

Place the flour in a bowl. Add 1½ pints boiling water. Allow the flour to absorb the water for 20 seconds, then mix well.

Boil 6 pints water and add salt. Divide the dough roughly into 8 round pieces and drop the *kachee* into the boiling water. Reduce heat to medium and cook for 20 minutes. Remove the *kachee* with a long-handled spoon and drain. Spread them in a large shallow dish no more than 1 inch deep. Cover with the yoghurt and pour over the butter. The *kachee* are ready to serve.

Mantu

Stuffed, steamed pasta

Serves 8   Preparation time: 1 hour

Mantu is a traditional Uzbeki dish which is now eaten throughout Afghanistan. In Afghanistan we cook *mantu* in a three-tiered steamer of cylindrical shape. A large western-style steamer will make a suitable alternative.

For the filling
1 lb (450 g) minced lamb
2 lb (900 g) onions
1 tsp black pepper
1 tsp salt

Mix all the ingredients together and leave to one side.

For the topping
3 tbsp (45 ml) oil
1 medium onion, peeled and finely chopped
15 oz (425 g) tinned peeled tomatoes
½ tsp salt
½ tsp chilli powder
15 oz (425g) yoghurt
3 cloves garlic, well crushed

Heat the oil. Fry the onion for 3 minutes. Add the tomatoes, salt and chilli powder, bring to the boil and simmer until the water has evaporated and the oil has separated out. Leave aside.

For the dough
1 lb (450 g) strong white flour
8 oz (225 g) plain flour
1½ tsp natural yoghurt
1½ tsp salt
¾ pint (425 ml) water
2 tbsp (30 ml) oil (for preparing dough)

Mix all ingredients well and knead for 5 minutes. The dough should be firm. Divide into 15 balls and leave to rest for 5 minutes.

Roll out each ball to about 2 mm thick and cut as many 5-cm (2-inch) squares as possible from each piece of dough.

To cook
Taking one piece of dough at a time, place ½ tbsp filling in centre of dough. Bring the four corners together to form a peak. Seal the adjoining edges of dough by pressing edges firmly together, making four seams, then press the opposite ends firmly together at the base. Put on a floured tray. Continue until all the *mantu* are prepared. Cover with a clean cloth and leave to one side.

Brush the inside bases of the steaming tiers or baskets with oil. Place the *mantu* in a single layer, leaving space around each *mantu*. Lightly brush the top of each *mantu* with oil.

Cover the steamer and steam the *mantu* for 20 minutes. Then leave to cool for 15 minutes before preparing to serve.

Mix crushed garlic with ½ cup yoghurt and spread on a large oval dish, arranging the cooked *mantu* in a single layer. Spread with the remainder of the yoghurt, then add the warmed topping.

Garnish with chopped coriander or parsley.

Maushawa

Yoghurt and pulses soup

Serves 8   Preparation time: 1 hour 30 minutes

This soup can be made with or without meatballs.

4 oz (110 g) split peas
4 oz (110 g) white kidney beans
8 oz (225 g) chickpeas
4 oz (110 g) yellow split peas
4 oz (110 g) mung beans
8 oz (225 g) short-grained rice
8 oz (225 g) wheat
½ tsp salt

Soak the split peas, white kidney beans, chickpeas, split peas and mung beans overnight.

In a pan, cover the ingredients with water. Bring to the boil and simmer until all the pulses are soft. Drain well.

9 tbsp (135 ml) oil
8 cloves garlic, finely chopped
1 large onion, finely chopped
½ pint (280 ml) tomato juice
2 pints (1·1 l) stock
1 tsp salt
½ tsp black pepper
¼ tsp turmeric
15 oz (425 g) Greek-style yoghurt

Juice of 1 lemon
½ tsp dried mint
2 green chillies, de-seeded and finely chopped
Chopped green peppers to garnish

Heat the oil in a heavy saucepan. Sauté the garlic and onion until light golden brown. Add the tomato juice and cook for a further 2 minutes, stirring continuously. When the oil starts to separate out, add the stock. Bring to the boil and add the cooked bean mixture. Cover and cook for 10 minutes. Add the salt, black pepper and turmeric. (Add the meatballs at this stage if you are using them.)

Put the yoghurt in a bowl. Add the lemon juice and sprinkle with dried mint. Add to the soup, stir slowly and after 3 minutes it will be ready to serve.

Garnish with the chopped green peppers.

For the meatballs (optional)
1½ lb (700 g) finely minced beef or lamb
1 medium onion, finely chopped
1 tsp salt
½ tsp freshly ground black pepper
1 tbsp dried coriander
1 tbsp fresh coriander, finely chopped

Combine all the ingredients and mix very well. Shape into balls the size of a hazelnut.

For the sauce
6 tbsp (90 ml) oil
1 medium onion, finely chopped
½ pint (280 ml) water
¼ tsp turmeric
½ tsp salt
¼ pint (140 ml) tomato juice
¼ pint (140 ml) stock

Heat the oil in a large, heavy-based saucepan. Sauté the onions until light golden. Add water, turmeric, salt and meatballs. Bring to the boil.

Cover and cook over a medium flame until the water has evaporated. Add the tomato juice. Cook until the oil separates out.

Add the stock, cover and simmer until tender.

Add meatballs and sauce to the soup before stirring in the yoghurt.

Pakaura

Deep-fried dishes

Each serves 8   Preparation time: 35 minutes

There are many kinds of *pakaura*, and they are very popular with vegetarians. Sliced aubergine, cauliflower florets, fish, chilli peppers and rhubarb can be cooked by this method. Here are three batters to use with different ingredients.

Potato pakaura
4½ oz (125 g) yellow split pea flour
4½ oz (125 g) chapati flour
¼ pint (140 ml) water
1 egg yolk
½ tsp bicarbonate of soda
1½ tsp salt
1 tbsp chilli powder
2 garlic cloves, crushed
1½ lb (700 g) potatoes, peeled and cut into thin, round slices
1 pint (550 ml) oil for frying

Mix the flours and water well together. Beat in the egg yolk, soda, salt, chilli powder and garlic. Add the potato slices and coat each one individually.

Heat ½ inch oil in a frying pan and add the coated potato slices in a single layer. Fry, turning when golden, to cook on the other side. Remove with a slotted spoon, allowing excess oil to drip back into pan. Repeat until all the coated potato slices have been cooked.

Serve hot with coriander chutney (p. 248).

Fish pakaura
1½ lb (700 g) fish 2–3 inches long, with heads and
    tails carefully removed.
1 egg yolk
4½ oz (125 g) chickpea flour
4½ oz (125 g) chapati flour
1½ tsp salt
¼ tsp bicarbonate of soda
½ tsp chilli powder
½ pint (280 ml) water
Juice of one small lemon
1 tbsp freshly chopped coriander
Corn or vegetable oil for frying

Follow the same cooking method as for potato *pakaura*, adding the lemon juice and coriander to the batter in place of the garlic.

Serve with coriander chutney.

Rhubarb pakaura
1½ oz (40 g) chickpea flour
1½ oz (40 g) plain flour
1 egg
1 tsp salt
½ tsp red chilli powder
½ pint (280 ml) water
½ tsp baking powder
1 lb (450 g) rhubarb, cut into slices
oil for frying

Follow the same cooking method as for potato *pakaura*. Serve with coriander chutney or lemon juice.

Sambosa-e-Uzbeki

Fried, stuffed pastries

Serves 8   Preparation time: 45 minutes

Sambosas can have either a meat or vegetable filling.

For the batter
1½ lb (700 g) strong flour
1 tsp dried yeast
½ tsp sugar
1 tsp salt
1 pint (550 ml) lukewarm milk
1 tbsp butter

Mix all the ingredients together and knead to form a dough. Cover with a cloth and leave in a warm place for 20 minutes.

For the filling
2 lb (900 g) onions, roughly chopped
2 tsp oil
1 lb (450 g) minced meat *or* chopped vegetables
1 tsp salt
2 tsp dried coriander
3 tsp black pepper
¼ tsp turmeric

Heat the oil and sauté the onions until they are transparent. Add the meat or vegetables, salt, coriander, pepper and turmeric. Brown, stirring well. Leave to one side.

To cook

Divide the dough into about 30 balls, 2 inches in diameter. Roll each one out to form a 4-inch circle. Spread 1 tbsp filling over the upper half of dough, without covering the outer edge. Fold the bottom half over the filling and press the edges together firmly.

Heat the oil in a frying pan and fry the *sambosas* over a medium heat until they are golden-brown on each side. Dry on kitchen paper, and serve hot or cold.

Kofta

Meatballs with tomato sauce

Serves 8   Preparation time: 1 hour

1½ lb (700 g) minced lamb (or use beef or mutton)
Few sprigs fresh coriander
4 cloves garlic
2 green chillies, de-seeded
1½ lb (700 g) onions, peeled and finely chopped
15 cardamom pods
1 egg
1 tsp salt
1 tbsp dried coriander
1 tsp cumin
6 tbsp (90 ml) corn oil
1 tsp grated ginger
7 oz (200 g) peeled, tinned tomatoes
1 tsp tomato purée
¾ pint (425 ml) chicken or beef stock
1 tsp black pepper

Mince the lamb, fresh coriander, garlic, chillies and 1 lb of the onions in a food processor until you have a fine-textured mixture.

Grind the coriander and cumin and 10 of the cardamom pods to a powder; add to the meat mixture with the egg and salt. Mix well by hand. Leave to one side while you prepare the sauce.

Heat the oil. Sauté the remaining onion until it is transparent. Add the ginger, tomatoes and tomato purée. Fry for approximately 5 minutes, until the oil separates out. Leave to cool a little and purée in blender. Return to the saucepan, add the stock, then lower the heat so that it is just on the boil.

Divide the meat mixture into 14 pieces and mould into balls. Drop them one at a time into the boiling sauce. Cover and simmer on a low heat for 15 minutes, by which time the water should have evaporated. Sprinkle in the whole cardamom pods and the ground black pepper.

Increase the heat to medium and gently stir the *kofta* and sauce for 5 minutes. Mix well so that sauce and *kofta* take on the same colour – a reddish brown. This last step gives Afghan *kofta* its unique character.

Kebab-e-bal morgh

Chicken wing kebabs

Serves 8   *Preparation time: 45 minutes (and 1 hour for marinade)*

2 lb (900 g) chicken wings (upper part of wings)
5 cloves garlic, finely chopped
1½ tsp salt
1 walnut-sized piece ginger, crushed
¼ tsp turmeric
¼ pint (140 ml) lemon juice or vinegar
½ tsp red chilli powder
¼ tsp cumin
3 tbsp (45 ml) oil
Small bunch fresh parsley or coriander

Skin the wings and wash them. Mix all the ingredients except the oil and marinate the chicken for 1 hour.

Heat the oil on a medium heat and fry the chicken for 10 minutes. Cover, and leave on a very low heat for 20 minutes.

Garnish with fresh parsley or coriander leaves.

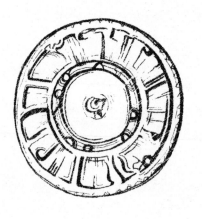

Dolmas Stuffed dishes

Dolma morgh Stuffed chicken

Dolma-e-morch-e-shireen Stuffed peppers

Morgh shkampor Chicken stuffed with nuts

Dolma-e-tokhom Savoury pancakes

Dolma morgh

Stuffed chicken

Serves 4–6   Preparation time: 45 minutes

1½ lb (700 g) chicken breasts
1 tbsp chicken seasoning *or*
    1 tsp chilli powder
    1 tsp garlic powder
    ½ tsp salt
Juice of 1 lemon
1 small onion, peeled and grated

Flatten each chicken breast or cut it horizontally in
half if it is thick. This should provide 6 slices of
chicken breast. Rub the chicken with the seasoning, lemon juice and onion and leave to marinate
for 2 hours.

For the filling
Small bunch fresh coriander
Small bunch continental parsley
10 cloves garlic
2 oz (60 g) unsalted butter
1 tsp freshly ground black pepper
1 tsp salt

Wash the coriander and parsley well and chop
finely with the garlic. Melt the butter and add to
the herbs, together with salt and pepper. Mix very
well.

To cook
2 eggs
Pinch salt
Breadcrumbs
Oil for deep-frying
Juice of ½ orange

Place 1 dessertspoonful of filling on each chicken breast and roll up, securing with wooden skewers if necessary.

Beat the eggs with a pinch of salt. Roll the *dolmas* in egg and then in breadcrumbs.

Heat the oil in a deep-fryer and cook the chicken for about 5 minutes, until it is golden brown.

Sprinkle with the orange juice and serve.

Dolma-e-morch-e-shireen

Stuffed peppers

Serves 6   Preparation time: 1 hour 30 minutes

1 lb (450 g) chicken breasts
1 medium onion, peeled and grated
2 tbsp olive oil
2 tbsp tomato purée
1 tsp freshly grated ginger
1½ tsp salt
3 oz (85 g) basmati rice
½ pint (280 ml) water
3 tbsp corn oil
3 cloves garlic, peeled and crushed
1 tsp freshly ground black pepper
½ tsp chilli powder
Juice of 1 lemon
A few sprigs fresh coriander, finely chopped
10 green peppers or a mixture of green, red and
   yellow
9 oz (250 g) single cream

Gas Mark 9/245°C/470°F, then Gas Mark
   5/190°C/370°F

Cut the chicken into 2-inch squares and marinate
for 2–3 hours with the onion, olive oil, tomato
purée, ginger and half of the salt.
   Heat the oven.
   Wash the rice well. Boil the water, add the rice

and cook for 2½ minutes. Drain and leave to one side.

Heat the corn oil. Add the crushed garlic and fry for half a minute. Pour over the marinated chicken. Lower the heat of the oven and cook the chicken for 30 minutes. Remove from the oven (but leave the oven on), cool and chop into very small pieces. Add the black pepper, chilli powder, lemon juice, coriander, rice and remaining salt. Mix very well together.

Slice the tops off the peppers. De-seed, wash and dry them. Fill the peppers with the rice and chicken mixture and replace the tops. Rub them with oil on the outside.

Put the oiled and stuffed peppers on a baking tray in the oven for 30 minutes, by which time the tops should be slightly brown.

Pour 2 tsp cream into each stuffed pepper and serve.

Morgh shkampor

Chicken stuffed with nuts

Serves 6   Preparation time: 1 hour 30 minutes

2 lb (900 g) basmati rice
2 oz (50 g) almonds
2 oz (50 g) pistachios
2 oranges
9 tbsp (135 ml) oil
1 chicken weighing 3–3½ lb (1·5 kg)
7 oz (200 g) peeled tomatoes
1 tbsp salt
1½ tsp black pepper
½ tsp saffron, soaked or dissolved in hot water
1½ tsp ground cardamom
20 whole cardamoms
5 oz (135 g) black raisins
½ tsp *pelau masala* (p. xv)
1 tbsp cumin
½ tbsp ground coriander
8 oz (225 g) chopped onion

Soak the rice for 30 minutes before cooking with ½ tsp salt.

Soak the almonds and the pistachios separately in hot water, then peel and cut the pistachios into halves and the almonds into quarters.

Cut the oranges into quarters, remove flesh and pith and cut the peel into long thin slices. Boil in

½ pint water for 3 minutes, drain and boil in ½ pint fresh water for 3 minutes.

Heat 3 tbsp oil in a frying pan. Add the raisins, cardamoms, almonds, pistachios and orange peel. Fry for 3 minutes; cover the pan and leave on a very low heat for another 3 minutes, then leave to one side.

Heat the remaining oil in a large saucepan. Fry the whole chicken for 5 minutes on both sides. Add the onion and peeled tomatoes and fry for 10 minutes. Add the salt, black pepper, saffron and cardamom powder. Then add 1½ pints water, cover the saucepan and boil for 15 minutes. The chicken should then be soft but should not break up. Remove the chicken from the stock and leave it to cool.

Stuff the chicken with the mixture of pistachios, orange peel, almonds, raisins and cardamoms.

Measure the stock. It should make 1 pint (550 ml).

Boil 2½ pints water, add the rice, boil for 2½ minutes and then drain. Put the rice back into the saucepan. Add the *pelau masala*, cumin, coriander, black pepper and the chicken stock. Mix very slowly to avoid breaking the rice grains.

Put the stuffed chicken in the middle of the rice, piling rice over it, and steam for about 30 minutes.

Dolma-e-tokhom

Savoury pancakes

Serves 6   Preparation time: 45 minutes

For the batter
6 eggs
6 tbsp (90 g) plain flour
9 tbsp (135 ml) water
½ tsp salt
Knob of butter, the size of a walnut
2 tbsp lemon juice

Mix all the ingredients together in a large bowl or food processor until well blended. Leave aside.

For the filling
1 lb (450 g) minced shoulder of lamb
2 medium onions
2 cloves garlic, finely chopped
1 tsp black pepper
1 tsp salt
3 tbsp (45 ml) corn or vegetable oil
¼ pint (140 ml) chicken or beef stock

Gas Mark 5/190°C/370°F

Mince meat, garlic and 1 onion together until finely chopped. Add pepper and salt.
    Peel and slice the other onion. Heat the oil in a frying pan. Sauté the onion until light golden. Add

59

the meat and onion mixture and fry it until lightly browned (approximately 5 minutes).

Add the stock, cover and simmer for 10 minutes. The stock should be absorbed. Remove excess oil with a spoon and reserve for the sauce.

For the sauce
7 oz (200 g) tinned tomatoes
Juice of ½ lemon
1 clove garlic, crushed

Put the oil saved from the filling into a saucepan with the tomatoes, lemon juice and crushed garlic clove. Fry for 2 minutes. Leave to one side.

To cook
Take a large non-stick frying pan and oil it slightly. Pour 3 tbsp (45 ml) batter into the pan and tilt it gently so the pancake spreads to the size of a large side plate. When the pancake is cooked underneath, toss it and cook the other side. Put the cooked pancake aside and continue in the same way until all the batter is used up and you have a pile of pancakes, ready for filling.

Take 1 pancake and spread 2½ tbsp meat mixture in line about 1 inch wide across the bottom third of the pancake. Fold the pancake over the filling and continue to roll until the pancake is completely rolled up. Repeat with all the pancakes.

Place the rolled pancakes side by side in an oven-proof dish. They may be cut into 2 or 3 if so desired. Pour on the sauce and place in a warm oven for 5–10 minutes.

Garnish with chopped parsley or coriander and serve with salad or on their own.

Qorma Rich stews with fruit, meat and vegetables

Qorma-e-saib Apple stew

Qorma-e-banjan Aubergine stew

Qorma-e-turraie Courgette and chicken stew

Qorma-e-gosht-e-gosphand Lamb stew

Qorma-e-samarok Mushroom stew

Qorma-e-alo bokhara wa dal nakhod Plum stew with yellow split peas

Qorma-e-kachalow Potato stew

Kofta ba rawash Minced meat with rhubarb

Qorma-e-sabzi Spinach stew

Qorma-e-tarkori Parsley and celery stew

Qorma-e-karam Cabbage stew

Qorma-e-morgh ba limmo Chicken drumsticks with lemon

Qorma-e-bamia Okra stew

Qorma

Qorma is the dish traditionally served with *chalau* rice (p. 135) and one of the dishes which make up the spread for a festive meal. It is a very rich meat-based stew, cooked either with vegetables or fruit.

In choosing your meat, it is essential that the fat and bone are used, as they give the full flavour and richness unique to *qorma*.

An important stage in the preparation of *qorma* is to cook the ingredients until the water has evaporated and oil separates out.

For best results, always fry the meat in oil for at least 5 minutes to remove excess fat. Add the chopped onions and fry for a further 5 minutes. Then add 1 cup water and fry for 8 minutes. Pour in 1½ pints water, cover the dish and leave over a medium heat for 25–30 minutes, until all the water has been absorbed. Depending on the vegetable ingredients used, some *qorma* dishes may require the addition of extra water or stock to prevent them from drying out too quickly. Variations on this method are given in individual recipes.

Qorma-e-saib

Apple stew

Serves 6–8   Preparation time: 45 minutes

8 oz (225 g) onion, peeled and chopped finely
1½ lb (700 g) shoulder or leg of lamb, cut into
    1½-inch cubes
¼ pint (140 ml) corn or vegetable oil
Juice of 1 lemon
1 tsp sugar
1 tsp salt
2 lb (900 g) cooking apples, peeled and cut into
    quarters
1 pinch powdered saffron

Heat the oil in a heavy-based saucepan. Sauté the
onions until light golden-brown.

Add meat and fry over high flame until lightly
browned (approximately 5 minutes). Stir in the
lemon juice, sugar and salt and cook for 1 minute.
Add 1 pint (550 ml) water and bring to the boil.
Cover and cook for about 25 minutes, until tender.

Add apples and saffron. Pour in 2½ fl oz (65 ml)
water and leave on a low heat for 5 minutes, until
the water has evaporated and the oil separates out.

Serve with *chalau* (p. 135) and salad.

Cherry *qorma* can be made in the same way,
using 2 lb (900 g) red cherries instead of the apples.

Qorma-e-banjan

Aubergine stew

Serves 4–6   Preparation time: 1½–2 hours

6 tbsp (90 ml) corn oil
1 large onion or 2 medium-sized onions, sliced
  vertically
1½ tsp salt
2 green chillies, de-seeded and roughly chopped
¼ tsp turmeric
1 beef or chicken stock cube
1 tsp chilli powder (optional)
2 lb (900 g) lamb on the bone cut into 1½-inch
  pieces
1½ lb (700 g) tomatoes skinned and chopped
  roughly
2 lb (900 g) aubergine, skinned and cut into 1-inch
  cubes
3 cloves garlic, crushed

Heat the oil and fry the onions until they are light
golden-brown. Add the salt, green chilli, turmeric,
stock cube and chilli powder. Stir for 1 minute.
Add the meat pieces, and fry gently until lightly
browned. Stir in the tomatoes and cook on a low
heat until soft, then add the aubergine. Simmer for
30 minutes, stirring slowly from time to time.
When the aubergine is browned, turn the heat
down very low for 5–10 minutes and the oil will
separate out.

Banjan bata (Aubergine stew without meat)
Heat the oil and sauté the onions until light golden. Add ¼ pint (140 ml) water, salt, chilli powder, turmeric, a beef stock cube and the aubergine. Continue to cook for 15 minutes. Add the tomatoes and cook for 20 minutes, or until the water has evaporated and the oil separates out. Serve with short-grained rice – *bata* (p. 156).

Qorma-e-turraie

Courgette and chicken stew

Serves 4–6   Preparation time: 40 minutes

6 tbsp (90 ml) oil
1½ lb (700 g) courgettes, in 1-inch pieces
1 medium onion, chopped
2 lb (900 g) skinned chicken
2 cloves garlic
¼ tsp turmeric or saffron
2 green chillies, finely chopped
1½ tsp salt
3 sticks celery, cut into 1-inch lengths
1 large green pepper and 1 large red pepper, cut
   into 1-inch pieces
1 pint (550 ml) chicken stock
Juice of 1 lemon
A few sprigs fresh coriander
½ tsp black pepper

Wash chicken and cut into 8 pieces.

Heat the oil in a medium saucepan. Add the courgettes and fry for 6 minutes. Remove the courgettes from the oil and keep to one side.

Fry the chopped onion in the oil for 5 minutes. Add the chicken and fry until it is golden-brown. Add the garlic, turmeric, green chillies, salt, celery and both peppers. Fry for 2 minutes. Add the stock and simmer until the chicken is tender and the water has evaporated. Cook for 2–3 more minutes, stirring gently all the time.

Add the courgettes, lemon juice, coriander and black pepper. Cover the saucepan and simmer gently for another 10 minutes.

Serve with plain white rice – *chalau* (p. 135).

Qorma-e-gosht-e-gosphand

Lamb stew

Serves 5   Preparation time: 1 hour 20 minutes

Chicken qorma (*Lawung qorma*) can be cooked in the same way, using chicken pieces instead of lamb.

6 tbsp (90ml) corn or vegetable oil
1 lb (450 g) onions, peeled and chopped finely
2 lb (900 g) leg of lamb on the bone cut into 1½-inch cubes
2 cloves garlic, peeled and crushed
1 tsp grated fresh ginger
3 green chillies, chopped
1½ tsp salt
¼ tsp turmeric
1 pint (550 ml) water (or ¾ pint water and ¼ pint stock)
¼ tsp freshly ground black pepper
5 whole cardamoms
A few sprigs fresh coriander, finely chopped
Juice of 1 small lemon
Small carton sour cream or double cream

Heat the oil in a large, heavy-based saucepan and sauté the onions over a medium flame until they are light golden-brown (approximately 10 minutes).

   Add meat and sauté over a medium flame until

lightly browned, adding the garlic, ginger, chillies and salt after 5 minutes. Sauté for a further 5 minutes.

Add half the water. Cook for 10 minutes, then add the turmeric and the rest of the water. Cover and simmer until the meat is tender (approximately 40 minutes).

Remove the lid, pour off the stock into a container, add the black pepper and fry the *qorma* gently for 3 minutes. Add the stock and cardamoms and leave on a low flame until you are ready to serve the *qorma*.

Garnish with the coriander, lemon juice and soured cream if desired. Serve with *chalau* (p. 135) or *naun* (p. 3).

Qorma-e-samarok

Mushroom stew

Serves 4   Preparation time: 30 minutes

6 tbsp (90 ml) oil
1 small onion
1 lb (450 g) boneless meat (lamb, chicken or beef)
2 lb (900 g) fresh mushrooms
Pinch of saffron
½ tsp salt
½ tsp ground red pepper or 1 green chilli

Slice the onion very finely and fry until very lightly browned.

Cut the meat into 1-inch cubes. Add to the onion and fry for 4 to 5 minutes.

Cut the mushrooms into 1 inch pieces. Wash thoroughly and add to the meat and onion, stirring occasionally. Add the saffron, then the salt and pepper. Keep on stirring until the mixture has turned golden-brown then reduce the heat. Add a little water if necessary, but there should already be enough moisture in the mushrooms.

Continue to simmer on a low heat until all the water has evaporated and then for not more than 5 minutes. Cover and simmer for a further 5 minutes.

Garnish as you wish and serve.

Qorma-e-alo bokhara wa dal nakhod

Plum stew with yellow split peas

Serves 6   Preparation time: 2 hours

4 oz (110 g) yellow split peas, soaked overnight
6 tbsp (90 ml) oil
1 lb (450 g) onions, peeled and finely chopped
2 lb (900 g) boned shoulder of lamb, cut into 1½-
   inch cubes
2 cloves garlic, peeled and finely chopped
1½ tsp salt
1 green chilli, de-seeded and finely chopped
½ tsp freshly ground pepper
⅛ tsp turmeric
10 whole green cardamoms
8 oz (225 g) purple plums, stoned
1½ tsp sugar (optional)
Juice of ½ lemon

Leave the split peas to soak in cold water for 1
hour and then drain.

Heat the oil in a heavy-based saucepan and sauté
the onions until golden. Add the meat, garlic and
salt to onion and fry until golden-brown (approximately 10 minutes). Add the chilli, pepper, turmeric, and cardamom, and stir for 1 minute. Add
1 pint (550 ml) water and bring to the boil. Cover,
and cook over a medium flame until the meat is
tender.

Add the split peas, plums, sugar (if desired) and lemon juice and cook over a low flame until the split peas are soft and the water is evaporated and the oil separates out.

Serve with *chalau* (p. 135) and salad.

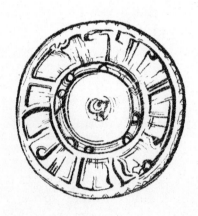

Qorma-e-kachalow

Potato stew

Serves 6–8   *Preparation time: 1 hour*

1½ lb (700 g) medium-sized potatoes
6 tbsp (90 ml) oil
3 cloves garlic
2 green chillies, finely chopped
6 tbsp Greek yoghurt
¼ tsp turmeric
½ tsp salt
Juice of ½ lemon

Peel the potatoes and cut them into quarters.

Heat the oil in a large frying pan and fry the garlic for ½ minute. Add the potatoes, chillies, turmeric, salt and lemon juice and fry for 5 minutes. Cover, and simmer for a further 5–10 minutes until the potatoes are cooked. Add some water if necessary.

Garnish with Greek yoghurt, and serve with *naun* (p. 3) and *chalau* (p. 135).

Kofta ba rawash

Minced meat with rhubarb

Serves 6   Preparation time: 45 minutes

1½ lb (700 g) boneless lamb or beef with fat
1½ lb (700 g) onions
3 cloves garlic
1 piece fresh ginger, walnut-sized
¼ tsp saffron, soaked or dissolved in hot water
2 fresh green chillies
1 tsp salt
1 egg
¼ tsp cinnamon
¼ tsp ground black cardamom
1½ tbsp dried coriander
½ tsp chilli powder
6 tbsp (90 ml) oil
1 pint (550 ml) hot water
1 lb (450 g) rhubarb
½ lb (225 g) tomatoes
4 tbsp plain yoghurt
1 tsp ground green cardamom

Mince the meat twice, with half the onion and garlic, the green chillies and ginger. Add the salt, egg, cinnamon, black cardamom, half the coriander, chilli powder and mix well.

Heat the oil in a medium saucepan, add the rest of the onion, and fry until golden-brown. Remove from the oil, leave to cool and then purée.

75

Add the rest of the crushed garlic to the oil and fry for 20 seconds. Add 1 pint (550 ml) hot water, the onion purée and the remaining coriander. Leave on a medium heat to simmer. After 15 minutes add the rhubarb and cook for a further 15 minutes.

Divide the meat into several balls, slightly bigger than eggs and then flatten them to make 3-inch patties. Add them to the sauce, with the chopped tomatoes, yoghurt and ground green cardamom. Leave on a low heat until the water has evaporated and oil separates out.

Serve with *chalau* rice (p. 135).

Qorma-e-sabzi

Spinach stew

Serves 6   Preparation time: 50 minutes

9 tbsp (135 ml) corn or vegetable oil
8 oz (225 g) onion, peeled and chopped finely
1½ lb (700 g) shoulder or leg of lamb, cut into
    1½-inch cubes
4 green chillies, de-seeded and finely chopped
1 tsp salt
¼ tsp turmeric
Juice of 1 lemon
1 bunch spring onions, peeled and finely chopped
4 bunches spinach, washed well and finely
    chopped
1 bunch coriander, washed well and finely
    chopped
1 tsp pepper
1 pint (550 ml) stock

Heat the oil in a heavy-based saucepan. Fry the onions for 4 minutes. Add the meat, green chillies, salt and turmeric and fry over a high flame for 5 minutes, until the mixture is a light golden-brown. Stir in the lemon juice, spring onions and coriander and cook for 3 minutes. Add the stock and bring to the boil.

Add the spinach and the pepper and mix well. Cover and cook for a further 15 minutes over a medium heat until all the water has evaporated and the oil separates out. Then remove the lid and cook for a further 5 minutes, stirring from time to time.

Serve hot with *chalau* rice (p. 135).

Qorma-e-tarkori

Parsley and celery stew

Serves 6   Preparation time: 1 hour

12 tbsp (180 ml) oil
1 medium onion, peeled and finely chopped
1½ lb (700 g) shoulder of lamb, cut into 1½-inch
  cubes
Juice of 1 lemon
1½ bunches parsley, washed and finely chopped
1 tsp dried mint
1 bunch celery, washed, scraped and cut into 1-
  inch pieces
1 tsp freshly ground black pepper
1½ tsp salt
1 pint (550 ml) water
Knob of butter

Heat 6 tbsp oil in a frying pan. Add the finely chopped onion and sauté until light golden-brown. Add the meat and sauté over a medium flame until lightly browned. Stir in the lemon juice and cook for 1 minute. Add ½ pint (280 ml) water and bring to the boil. Cover and cook until tender.

In another frying pan, heat 3 tbsp oil. Add the parsley and gently fry for 5 minutes. Heat 3 tbsp oil and sauté the celery for 5 minutes. Add to the meat mixture with the pepper, salt and ½ pint (280 ml) water. Fry the mint for 1 minute then add to the meat and mix well. Simmer gently for 30 minutes.

Serve with *chalau* rice (p. 135) or *naun* (p. 3).

Qorma-e-karam

Cabbage stew

Serves 6   Preparation time: 1 hour

This dish can be prepared without meat as a vegetarian dish.

6 tbsp (90 ml) oil
¼ tsp turmeric
2 medium onions
1 tsp fresh ginger
1 green chilli
2 cloves garlic
2 tsp salt
1½ lb (700 g) lamb
7 oz (200 g) chopped tomatoes
½ pint (280 ml) water
1 medium cabbage, chopped
Small bunch or 3 oz (85 g) fresh green coriander
Juice of 1 lemon

Heat the oil in a heavy-based saucepan and fry the chopped onion until it is a light golden-brown. Then add the fresh ginger, green chilli, garlic, salt and meat. Fry for 6 minutes.

Add the tomatoes and cook for 3 minutes. Add ½ pint (280 ml) water, cover the pan and continue to cook until the meat is slightly tender.

Stir in the chopped cabbage, fresh coriander and lemon juice. Cover, and leave to simmer on a low heat for 30 minutes until all the water has evaporated. Stir gently and serve with *chalau* rice or *naun*.

Qorma-e-morgh ba limmo

Chicken drumsticks with lemon

Serves 3   Preparation time: 1 hour

6 tbsp (90 ml) corn or vegetable oil
6 chicken drumsticks
1 medium onion, peeled and vertically sliced
3 cloves garlic, finely chopped
1 tsp salt
1 green chilli, halved and de-seeded
1 tsp fresh ginger, grated
¼ tsp turmeric
¾ pint (425 ml) water
1 large lemon cut into wedges and juice of ½
  lemon
1 tsp sugar
½ tsp ground cinnamon
10 whole cardamoms

Fry the chicken legs in the oil until they are brown.
Remove them from the pan and fry the onion until
light golden. Add the chicken, garlic, salt, chilli,
ginger and turmeric. Fry for 2 minutes, add ½ pint
(280 ml) water and simmer until the chicken is
tender.

Bring ¼ pint (140 ml) water to the boil. Add
the lemon wedges, simmer until tender and then
drain. Remove the lemon peel and discard the rest.

Take ¼ pint (140 ml) chicken stock from the
frying pan. Add the lemon peel, sugar, cinnamon,

cardamom and lemon juice. Simmer in a small pan for 5 minutes. Pour over the chicken and serve with *chalau* rice (p. 135).

Another chicken and lemon *qorma* is the Uzbeki version. Here the meat is cooked in the usual way in oil until tender. Then, at the stage when the spices are added, lemon rings are arranged between the meat pieces and the *qorma* is cooked for a further 10 minutes.

Qorma-e-bamia

Okra stew

Serves 4–6   Preparation time: 45 minutes

Qorma-e-bamia is prepared as a main dish either with meat or as a vegetarian dish with the meat omitted. It is well known as an aid to easy digestion.

1 lb (450 g) okra
6 tbsp (90 ml) oil
1 medium onion, finely chopped
1 lb (450 g) lamb or beef, cut into small cubes
1 clove garlic, crushed
1 tsp salt
2 small green chillies
2 small tomatoes, chopped
Juice of 1 small lemon

Wash and dry the okra and trim carefully without allowing juices to escape.

Heat the oil and fry the okra for 6 minutes on medium heat, stirring gently to avoid breaking the okra. Separate from the oil and keep to one side.

Using the same oil, fry the chopped onion until it just starts to turn golden. Add the meat, garlic, salt, green chillies and fry for 5 more minutes.

Add the chopped tomatoes and cook until they start to soften. Add a cup of water and simmer until meat is tender. Add the okra and mix in gently. Then add the lemon juice, cover and simmer gently for 15 minutes. Serve with rice or *naun* (p. 3).

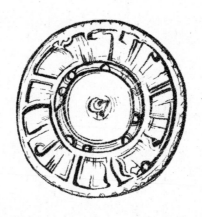

Mahi Fish dishes

Qorma-e-mahi Fish curry

Mahi wa gashneez Fish with coriander

Kebab-e-mahi sikhi Fish kebab

Mahi

In Afghanistan, only freshwater fish is available. It is popular all year round, but it is mostly eaten in the winter time. It can be prepared in many exciting ways. In this book we give you only a few examples.

Qorma-e-mahi

Fish curry

Serves 6   Preparation time: 45 minutes

2 lb (900 g) trout
2 cups (360 ml) oil
¾ lb (340 g) onions
1 lb (450 g) tinned, peeled tomatoes
1 tsp chilli powder
1 tsp salt
1 tsp ground coriander
3 cloves garlic
1 tsp grated fresh ginger
¼ tsp turmeric
1 pint (550 ml) water
1 lb (450 g) chinese radish
Juice of 1 lemon

Gut the fish, remove head and tail and cut into 3-inch pieces.

Heat the oil in a large saucepan and fry the fish on both sides until lightly browned.

Peel the onions and cut them with thin strips. Fry in the same oil until light golden-brown. Add the tomatoes, salt and spices and fry until the oil separates out.

Add 1 pint (550 ml) water and cook on a medium heat.

Scrape the radish clean and cut horizontally into rounds ½ inch thick. Then cut the rounds into quarters. Boil in a separate saucepan until soft. Drain the radish and add to the curry, carefully leaving pieces of fish whole. Add the lemon juice.

Serve with *chalau* rice (p. 135).

Mahi wa gashneez

Fish with coriander

Serves 4   *Preparation time: 1 hour 15 minutes
(and 2–3 hours for the marinade)*

2 lb (900 g) white fish
5 cloves garlic
1 tsp tomato purée
1 tsp salt
Juice of 1 lemon
2 medium onions
½ bunch fresh coriander
1 tsp freshly ground black pepper
1 tsp freshly chopped coriander
3 knobs of butter
½ tsp chilli powder
Slices of tomato to decorate

Gas Mark 5/190°C/370°F

Mix the crushed garlic, tomato purée, chilli powder, salt and lemon juice. Rub well into the fish, and place in an ovenproof dish for 2–3 hours to marinate.

Finely slice the onion and coriander. Mix them together and place in a layer over the fish. Decorate with slices of tomato, dot with knobs of butter and cook for 1 hour, turning after 30 minutes. Sprinkle with pepper and coriander and serve.

Kebab-e-mahi sikhi

Fish kebab

Serves 8   *Preparation time: 45 minutes (and 6
hours for the marinade)*

3 lb (1350 g) salmon or medium-sized fish
  (weighed with bones)
5 cloves garlic, crushed
1½ tsp salt
1 tsp chilli powder
1 walnut-sized piece fresh ginger, grated
¼ pint (140 ml) vinegar or lemon juice
A few sprigs parsley or coriander to garnish

Clean and wash the fish. Dry them with kitchen
paper and remove heads and tails.

Make a marinade with the garlic, salt, chilli
powder, ginger and vinegar or lemon. Dip each
fish in the marinade and place it skin side down
in a dish, pressing gently along the backbone to
flatten out the fish. Repeat with the second fish
and place it on top of the first one, skin side up
this time. Continue to arrange the fish in pairs.
Pour the remaining liquid over the fish. Allow the
fish to marinate for at least 6 hours or overnight
before cooking.

Grill the fish with the skin side up until golden
brown, then turn over and repeat. Do not allow
the fish to dry out completely. Before serving, pour

lemon juice over the fish and garnish with parsley
or coriander.

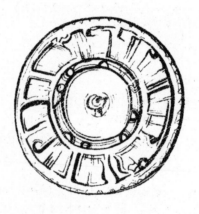

Kebabs

Kebab-e-maghz Brain kebab

Kebab-e-morgh Chicken kebab (i)

Kebab-e-morgh Chicken kebab (ii)

Kebab-e-morgh Chicken kebab (iii)

Kebab lolae morgh Stuffed chicken kebab

Pancake kebab

Kebab-e-dosh Oven kebab (i)

Kebab-e-diggee Oven kebab (ii)

Kebab-e-kaborgha Lamb cutlet kebab

Kebab-e-dolma-e-morgh Chicken roll

Kebab shikhi-e-jigar Liver kebab

Kebab-e-shomi Meatball kebab

Kebab ba chalau-e-shibet Kebab with dill chalau

Kebab-e-keema Deep-fried potato and meatballs

Raní gosphand Leg of lamb kebab

Kebab-e-morgh ba limmo Lemon chicken kebab

Lola kebab Beef roll

Kebab-e-tokhom Egg kebab

Kebab-e-ruye naun   Kebab with bread

Shushlik kebab-e-Uzbeki   Hot minced kebab

Kebab-e-kalpura   Sweetbread kebab

Kebab-e-dip-e-Uzbeki   Uzbeki kebab dip

Rhub-e-kebab   Kebab sauce

Kebab-e-maghz

Brain kebab

Serves 4   Preparation time: 30 minutes

Sheep's brains are a delicacy in Afghanistan and widely available. Ask your butcher to order them for you.

1 lb (450 g) brains
Salted hot water
12 tbsp (180 ml) corn or vegetable oil
1 small onion, chopped
¼ tsp turmeric
1 tsp salt
1 tsp black pepper
Juice of 1 lemon
1 egg, beaten lightly
6 oz (170 g) breadcrumbs
Fresh coriander or parsley to garnish

Soak the brains in hot salted water for a few hours, then skin them.

Boil the brains in 1½ pints (850 ml) water for 5 minutes with the onion, half the lemon juice and half of the salt and pepper. Drain.

Add the turmeric and the remaining salt and pepper to the beaten egg. Dip the brains in the egg mixture and coat with breadcrumbs. Heat the oil in a frying pan and fry the brains until they are golden on each side.

Garnish with a few fresh coriander or parsley leaves and sprinkle with the remaining lemon juice. Serve with *naun* (p. 3) and salad.

Kebab-e-morgh

Chicken kebab (i)

Serves 4   Preparation time: 30 minutes

8 chicken drumsticks
1 medium onion, finely chopped
¼ tsp turmeric
1 tsp salt
1 tsp pepper
1 pint (550 ml) water
3 cloves garlic
Juice of 1 lemon
Fresh coriander or parsley leaves to garnish

Put all the ingredients except the garlic and lemon juice in a saucepan. Bring to the boil, then simmer without stirring until tender. Taking care not to break the skin, remove the drumsticks from the liquid and grill gently until golden-brown on both sides.

Crush the garlic and mix with the lemon juice. Add a pinch of salt and sprinkle over the drumsticks, with little black pepper.

Garnish with coriander or parsley leaves and serve hot with *naun* (p. 3) and salad.

Kebab-e-morgh

Chicken kebab (ii)

Serves 6   *Preparation time: 30 minutes (and 3–4 hours for the marinade)*

3 lb (1350 g) chicken
1 pint (550 ml) milk
1 tsp salt
1 inch cinnamon stick
4 cloves
10 black peppercorns
10 whole cardamoms
10 oz (280 g) self-raising flour
½ tsp garlic powder
½ tsp black pepper
Oil for deep-frying
Lemon slices and finely chopped fresh coriander
   to garnish

Cut the chicken into 6 pieces. Make a marinade of the milk, 1 tsp of the salt, cardamoms, cinnamon, cloves and black peppercorns and marinate the chicken for 3–4 hours.

In a separate dish, mix together the flour, garlic powder, black pepper and the remaining salt. Leave to one side.

Place the chicken and marinade in a saucepan. Cook over a high flame until the chicken is slightly soft, or approximately 10 minutes. Strain the chicken, reserving the sauce. Leave the chicken to cool for 10 minutes.

Heat the oil in a deep frying pan. Dip the chicken pieces in the sauce, then roll them in flour. Fry until golden-brown.

Place on a heated serving dish, garnish with lemon slices and coriander and serve with any type of chutney, *naun* (p. 3) and a salad.

Kebab-e-morgh

Chicken kebab (iii)

Serves 6   *Preparation time: 1 hour (and 3–4 hours for the marinade)*

3 lb (1350 g) chicken
8 oz (225 g) grated onion
1 tbsp salt
1 tbsp black pepper
1 tsp grated fresh ginger
2 tbsp tomato purée
Juice of 1 lemon
2 tbsp olive oil
3 tbsp oil
4 cloves garlic

Gas Mark 7/220°C/430°F

Cut the chicken into 6 pieces. Marinate in onion, salt, black pepper, ginger, lemon juice and olive oil for 3–4 hours.

Heat the oil in a frying pan, add the crushed garlic and tomato purée and fry for 1 minute.

Cover the base of an ovenproof dish with foil. Remove chicken pieces from the marinade and place in the dish, spreading with the garlic mixture. Cover the chicken with foil and cook in the oven for 45 minutes.

Garnish with freshly chopped coriander or parsley and serve with a salad.

Kebab lolae morgh

Stuffed chicken kebab

Serves 4   Preparation time: 45 minutes

Medium bunch parsley
Medium bunch coriander
½ tsp freshly ground black pepper
½ tsp salt
1½ cloves garlic, crushed
½ egg
8 oz (225 g) fresh white breadcrumbs
1 tsp butter, finely sliced
2 walnuts, chopped
1 lemon
2 lb (900 g) chicken breast with skin
Tandoori masala (p. xv)

To make the stuffing, finely chop the parsley and
coriander. Add the pepper, salt, garlic, egg, breadcrumbs, butter and walnuts. Mix well together.

Remove the skin from the chicken breasts. Wash
and trim the skin.

Slice the chicken breasts horizontally into pieces
no more than ⅛ inch thick (approximately 4 inches
by 2 inches in size).

Cut the chicken skin to the same size. Lay out
pieces of skin with the inside facing upwards, and
dust them with a little *tandoori masala*. Put the sliced
chicken on top of the skin and dust it in the same
way. Then spread it with ½ tbsp stuffing mixture.

Roll up, securing the ends by skewering or sewing, so that the stuffing does not ooze out when cooking. Sprinkle with half the lemon juice.

Heat the oil in a frying pan. Cook the kebabs until golden-brown and place them in a warm serving dish. Sprinkle with the rest of the lemon juice and serve.

Pancake kebab

Serves 6   Preparation time: 1 hour

6 eggs
6 tbsp (90 g) flour
½ tsp salt
½ tsp black pepper
Pinch of baking powder
¼ pint (140 ml) water
2 lb (900 g) minced beef
1 lb (450 g) finely chopped onions
14 oz (425 g) tinned tomatoes
6 tbsp (90 ml) corn oil
½ pint (280 ml) stock
1½ tsp salt
1 green chilli, finely chopped
½ tbsp freshly crushed ginger
Oil for frying

Make a pancake batter by blending the eggs, flour, salt, pepper and water in a food processor or by hand. Leave to one side.

Heat the oil and sauté the onions until golden-brown. Add the meat and fry for 5 minutes. Add the tomatoes, ginger, chilli, salt and pepper and fry until the oil separates out. Add the stock, cover and simmer until the meat is tender and the oil separates out. Divide into 2 portions and leave to one side.

Heat a large frying pan. Add 1 tbsp oil. Pour in ½ cup of batter and cook gently until golden-brown. Toss the pancake and cook the other side. Put it on a plate and continue until all the batter is used up.

Using one portion of filling and all the pancakes, spread 2 tbsp filling over the centre of each pancake and roll up into cigar shapes. Place in an ovenproof dish. Spread the remaining filling mixture over the pancake kebabs. Cover with foil and put in low oven to warm through.

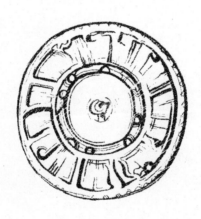

Kebab-e-dosh

Oven kebab (i)

Serves 4   Preparation time: 1 hour 20 minutes

1½ lb (700 g) onions
12 tbsp (180 ml) oil
2 lb (900 g) leg of lamb (including fat), cut in
  1-inch cubes
¼ tsp turmeric
2 cloves garlic
1 tsp freshly grated ginger
¼ tsp black pepper
1 tsp dried coriander
1½ tsp salt
1 chicken stock cube
½ cup (90 ml) lemon juice
2 green chillies, finely chopped

Gas Mark 4/180°C/355°F

Cut the onions into rings. Heat the oil in a heavy
ovenproof dish, add half the onions and fry for 5
minutes. Add the lamb and fry until golden-
brown, for approximately 7 minutes. Add the turmeric, ginger, garlic, pepper, dried coriander, salt
and the remaining onions. Cook for a further 5
minutes.

Transfer to an ovenproof dish. Dissolve the stock
cube in hot water and lemon juice and pour over
the kebab. Cover, and cook in the oven for 20

minutes. Remove the cover, turn the meat and cook for a further 10 minutes, or until golden-brown.

Serve with *naun* and a salad.

An alternative oven kebab is made of lamb pieces cooked between layers of onions, tomatoes, and green peppers. Fry the meat with some chopped onion first, arrange in layers with the vegetables and then cook in a covered dish in a slow oven for 40 minutes.

Kebab-e-diggee

Oven kebab (ii)

Serves 6   Preparation time: 1 hour

Kebab diggee is prepared from boneless meat. This dish has its origin in Paghman, which forms part of Greater Kabul. Paghman, a green and mountainous region, is also famous for its cherries and walnuts.

2 lb (900 g) boneless lamb
1½ lb (700 g) chopped onion
1 tbsp dried coriander
1 tsp black pepper
6 tbsp (90 ml) oil
Juice of 2 small lemons
2 tsp salt
½ pint (280 ml) tomato juice
Juice of 1 fresh orange
2 cloves garlic, crushed

Gas Mark 5/190°C/370°F

Cut the lamb into pieces 2 inches by 1½ inches. Place the lamb, onions, tomato juice and lemon juice in a heavy saucepan and simmer until the meat is tender, for 15 minutes.

Add the oil, black pepper, dried coriander, salt and garlic. Fry until light golden-brown. Add the orange juice and transfer the mixture to an ovenproof dish and cover. Place in the oven and cook for at least 25 minutes. Garnish with green vegetables.

Kebab-e-kaborgha

Lamb cutlet kebab

Serves 4   *Preparation time: 30 minutes (and 1 hour for the marinade)*

1½ tsp salt
1 tsp black pepper
1½ tsp chilli powder
4 tbsp (60 g) natural yoghurt
2 lb (900 g) lamb cutlets
Juice of 1 lemon and chopped coriander for
  garnish

Gas Mark 4/180°C/355°F, then Gas Mark
  6/205°C/400°F

Mix the salt, pepper, chilli powder and yoghurt and leave to one side for 15 minutes. Wash the cutlets and leave to marinate in the yoghurt mixture for 1 hour.

Place the cutlets in a greased roasting dish. Cook in the oven for 20 minutes, then increase the oven temperature and cook for 5 minutes on each side. The cutlets are cooked when they are light brown.

Sprinkle with lemon juice and garnish with chopped coriander.

Kebab-e-dolma-e-morgh

Chicken roll

Serves 6   *Preparation time: 1 hour (and 1 hour for the marinade)*

6 boned chicken legs
1½ tsp salt
3 green chillies, crushed
½ tsp turmeric
10 cloves garlic, crushed
2 tsp ginger, grated
A few sprigs fresh coriander or marjoram, finely
  chopped
¼ pt (140 ml) white vinegar
5 tbsp tomato purée
2 large red peppers
5 tbsp corn oil
½ tsp black pepper
1 orange
packet of toothpicks

Bone the chicken legs carefully, keeping the skin on, and leave to one side.

Put the salt, crushed green chillies, turmeric, garlic, ginger, vinegar and half of the black pepper in a large bowl and mix well. Take the legs one by one, dip them in the mixture on the fleshy side and coat well. Leave in a bowl to marinate for 1 hour.

Peel the orange, carefully discarding the pith,

and put the shredded peel in a little cold water to prevent drying out. Squeeze the orange and keep the juice to one side. Take the red peppers, steam them gently for about 5 minutes and shred ready for the garnish.

Take each boned, marinated leg and flatten it, skin side down. Sprinkle a portion of the orange juice, orange peel, and coriander or marjoram over the meat. Then starting at the narrower end, roll the meat, pulling the skin round as you go, and secure the roll with toothpicks or some fine string.

Mix the tomato purée with the oil and water, and put in a saucepan over a low heat. When heated through put in all the chicken rolls side by side and cover the pan. Leave on a low heat for 10 minutes, uncover and see that the water has all been absorbed, then turn the rolls over gently. Leave to cook for 10 more minutes, take off the heat and leave for 10–15 minutes to cool. Keeping the remainder of the liquid, place the rolls carefully under the grill and cook until well browned. Leave to cool.

With a sharp knife tilted at a slight diagonal, cut rolls into slices 1½ cm thick. Arrange slices on a flat dish, and reheat. (The rolls are easier to cut when cool.)

To serve, pour over the remaining liquid from the saucepan and garnish with the shredded red pepper and the remaining black pepper.

Kebab shikhi-e-jigar

Liver kebab

Serves 8   Preparation time: 1 hour (and 2 hours for marinade)

2lb (900 g) lamb's liver, cut into large pieces
   approx. 2 inches square
1½ tsp salt
½ tsp chilli powder
Few sprigs coriander, chopped
1 medium onion, grated
1 red pepper, coarsely chopped
1 green pepper, coarsely chopped
3 cloves garlic, crushed
2 tbsp (30 ml) natural yoghurt
2 tbsp (30 ml) corn or olive oil
Juice of 1½ lemons
1 medium onion, cut into rings
½ tsp black pepper
½ tsp ground coriander
1 tsp dried coriander

Mix the salt, chilli powder, ground coriander, grated onion, red and green peppers, yoghurt, oil and half the lemon juice. Marinate the liver for 2 hours.

Turn the grill on full. Using skewers or wooden skewer sticks, thread 2 pieces of marinated liver then 1 piece of pepper, leaving a slight space between, until the skewer is full.

Cook under the grill, turning from time to time until the kebabs are golden-brown.

To serve immediately
Sprinkle with lemon juice and dried coriander and garnish with fresh coriander.

To serve up to 30 minutes later
Remove the kebabs from the skewers and place in a warmed casserole. Sprinkle with lemon and dried coriander, cover, and keep on lowest possible heat. Garnish with fresh coriander when ready to serve.

Kebab-e-shomi

Meatball kebab

Serves 4   Preparation time: 45 minutes

1 lb (450 g) leg of lamb, boned
1 green chilli, de-seeded and finely chopped
1½ tsp salt
1 tsp black pepper
¼ tsp turmeric
½ lb (225 g) potatoes
10 whole cardamoms
2 tsp ground coriander
½ tsp ground ginger
A few sprigs fresh coriander, finely chopped
3–4 spring onions, finely chopped
1 small onion, chopped
3 cloves garlic, crushed
1 egg
Corn oil for deep frying

Boil the lamb for 10 minutes in 1 pint (550 ml) water with the green chilli, 1 tsp salt, black pepper and turmeric, until the water begins to evaporate. Leave aside to cool.

Boil the potatoes in their skins until soft. Peel and mash.

Mince the lamb and add the mashed potatoes, salt, remaining spices, chopped coriander, spring onions, chopped onion, garlic and egg. Knead well.

Keeping your palms moistened with oil, take about 2 tbsp of the mixture at a time. Make cigar shapes with half the mixture and shape the rest into balls.

Deep fry in the corn oil, on a medium heat.

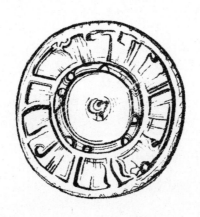

Kebab ba chalau-e-shibet

Kebab with dill chalau

Serves 5   Preparation time: 30 minutes

1 lb (450 g) very finely minced beef
1½ lb (700 g) grated potatoes, uncooked
Small bunch fresh coriander
1½ tbsp dried coriander
3 cloves garlic
½ tbsp salt
½ tbsp black pepper
1 medium onion, grated
Fresh ginger, walnut-sized, peeled and finely
  grated
2 tbsp flour
2 green chillies, finely chopped

Gas Mark 5/190°C/370°F

Mix all the ingredients very well together and
knead for 5 minutes.

Divide the mixture into larger than egg-shaped
pieces and flatten slightly.

Deep-fry the kebabs or oil them slightly and cook
in the oven, turning half way through.

Serve with dill *chalau* (p. 139) or a salad.

Kebab-e-keema

Deep-fried potato and meatballs

Serves 4   Preparation time: 1 hour

1½ lb (700 g) potatoes, peeled and grated
1 lb (450 g) finely minced beef or lamb
2 fresh green chillies, de-seeded and finely
  chopped
3 cloves garlic
1 tsp salt
1 tbsp ground cumin
1 tbsp dried coriander
½ tsp black pepper
Oil for frying

Gas Mark 5/190°C/370°F

Put the grated potatoes in a sieve and allow the juices to drain through for 5 minutes. Mix all the ingredients together thoroughly.

Divide the mixture into 20 and make sausage shapes. Deep-fry them one by one until golden-brown, or cook in the oven for 30 minutes.

Garnish with lemon juice and serve with a salad.

Raní gosphand

Leg of lamb kebab

Serves 8   *Preparation time: 1 hour 10 minutes
(and 6–8 hours for marinade)*

2½–3 lb (1135–1360 g) leg of lamb
2½ tsp salt
1½ tsp paprika
1 tsp chicken seasoning
5 cloves garlic, crushed
Juice of 2 large lemons
1½ tbsp dried coriander
2 knobs butter, walnut-sized
1 crushed onion
Juice of one orange
Lemon slices and parsley or coriander to garnish

Gas Mark 5/190°C/370°F

Wash the leg of lamb in warm water. Dry it with kitchen paper. Make several deep slits with a sharp knife. Mix all the ingredients (except the butter) and spread over the lamb, completely filling the incisions. Put the butter on top, wrap in foil and place in the refrigerator for 6–8 hours.

Still wrapped in the foil, bake the leg of lamb in the oven for 1 hour. The lamb should have turned a golden colour. If not, cook for another 15 minutes.

Garnish, and serve on a flat dish.

Kebab-e-morgh ba limmo

Lemon chicken kebab

Serves 6   Preparation time: 30 minutes

3 lb (1350 g) roasting chicken cut into 12 pieces
1 tsp salt
1 lemon and 1 tbsp lemon juice
6 tbsp (90 ml) oil
3 dessertspoons (45 g) sugar
½ tsp cinnamon
½ tsp turmeric
½ tsp curry powder
2 cloves garlic
1 tsp ground coriander
1 tsp black pepper
1 Spanish onion, sliced

Gas Mark 4/180°C/355°F

Rub the chicken pieces well with ½ tsp salt and the juice of half the lemon.

Heat the oil. Add the sugar and lightly brown. Add the cinnamon, turmeric and curry powder. Then add the chicken pieces and garlic. Fry until brown.

Add 5 tbsp (75 ml) water and the rest of the lemon, cut into slices. Cook for 5 minutes. Add the ground coriander.

Put the black pepper, salt, onion and 1 tbsp lemon juice into ¼ pint (140 ml) warm water. Cook until the onion is soft. Add to chicken. Cover and cook for a further 5 minutes.

Bake in the oven for 15 minutes, or until the top is golden-brown.

Lola kebab

Beef roll

Serves 6–8   *Preparation time: 1 hour 15 minutes*

1 red pepper
2 large onions
1 small bunch celery
1½ lb (700 g) minced beef
1½ tsp salt
1 tsp black pepper
2 eggs
½ tsp nutmeg
½ tsp cinnamon
1 tsp grated ginger or ground ginger
1 tsp ground coriander
4 oz (110 g) breadcrumbs
3 cloves garlic
2 oz (50 g) parsley
2 tbsp tomato purée
1 green pepper
Oil for frying
2 tsp lemon juice
1 beef stock cube
4 oz (110 g) mild cheddar cheese, grated

Gas Mark 4/180°C/355°F

Chop the red pepper, onion and 3 sticks of celery finely and mix with the meat in a large bowl. Add the salt, pepper, eggs, spices, breadcrumbs, garlic, parsley and tomato purée and mix thoroughly.

Roughly chop the green pepper, onion and remaining celery. Fry for 10 minutes. Add 1 tsp lemon juice and the beef stock cube dissolved in a little boiling water.

Take a piece of aluminium foil, approximately 18 inches square. Oil it well. Press the meat mixture into an oval shape approximately 9 inches at its widest. Spread with the fried vegetables and sprinkle with grated cheese. Gently fold so that the edges meet in the middle, then fold again. Put in a well-oiled loaf tin approximately 14 × 6 inches. Bake in the oven for 45 minutes.

Serve with chutney and salad.

Kebab-e-tokhom

Egg kebab

Serves 6   Preparation time: 1 hour

1 lb (450 g) lean beef, off the bone
½ lb onions
3 green chillies
2 tbsp dried coriander
1 tsp cumin
1 tbsp fresh ginger, crushed
½ tbsp salt
4 cloves garlic, crushed
Few sprigs fresh coriander
2 tbsp plain flour
10 eggs, hard-boiled
Parsley, celery and slices of lemon and tomato to
   garnish

Gas Mark 6/205°C/400°F

Put all the ingredients except the eggs in a food
processor and mince twice. Divide the mixture into
10 balls, flatten them and wrap around the eggs.

Grease a baking tray and arrange the egg balls
on it, leaving ½ inch between each ball. Cook in
the pre-heated oven for 30 minutes, until golden
brown.

Cut each ball in half and garnish with parsley,
celery, tomatoes and slices of lemon. Serve hot or
cold with chutney.

Kebab-e-ruye naun

Kebab with bread

Serves 6–8   *Preparation time: 45 minutes (and 4 hours for the marinade)*

2 lb (900 g) boneless veal or lamb with fat
15 oz (425 g) natural yoghurt
2 lb (900 g) onion, sliced thinly
6 tbsp (90 ml) corn oil
1½ lb (700 g) fresh tomatoes, sliced
½ tsp red pepper
½ tbsp salt
3 hot green chillies, finely chopped
5 cloves garlic
Juice of 1 fresh lemon
1 tsp black pepper
4 large pieces *naun* (p. 3)
Mint leaves to garnish

Wash the meat and dry it with kitchen paper. Cut into small cubes and marinate in the yoghurt, garlic, red pepper and salt for 4 hours.

Gently brown the meat in a saucepan until all the water evaporates.

Fry the onion in the corn oil for approximately 10 minutes. Add the green chillies and the tomatoes. Cook for 5 minutes.

Mix with the meat and add the black pepper and lemon juice. Leave for 15 minutes to cook over a low heat, keeping the frying pan covered.

Slice the bread into medium-sized pieces and place in flat dishes.

Spread the kebab on top and decorate with the mint leaves.

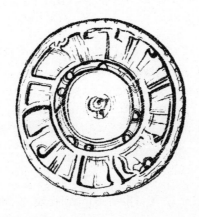

Shushlik kebab-e-Uzbeki

Hot minced kebab

Serves 6   Preparation time: 30 minutes

2 lb (900 g) minced lamb
5 garlic cloves, crushed
2 lb (900 g) onions, finely chopped
1 beaten egg
2 tsp salt

Mix all the ingredients in a bowl. Grease a large frying pan and place the mixture in it. Flatten the mince with a wooden spoon so that it covers the base of the pan. Cover, and place on a high heat. Cook for 10 minutes, agitating the pan occasionally.

Turn and mix the mince. Sprinkle with water and cook for a further 10 minutes, stirring from time to time.

Serve with rice and Uzbeki kebab dip (p. 126) or fried tomatoes.

Kebab-e-kalpura

Sweetbread kebab

Serves 4   Preparation time: 30 minutes

1 large onion, finely sliced
9 tbsp (135 ml) oil
2 lb (900 g) sweetbreads
1 tsp salt
2 tbsp natural yoghurt
½ tsp grated fresh ginger
¼ tsp turmeric
¼ tsp ground coriander
¼ tsp black pepper
2 cloves garlic, crushed
1 tomato, quartered
A handful of finely chopped coriander or parsley

Fry the onion until it is light brown (for approximately 8 minutes).

Wash and peel the sweetbreads. Cut each in half, add the salt and fry with the onion until golden-brown. (This takes a little time – stir frequently.)

Stir in the yoghurt, ginger, turmeric, ground coriander, black pepper and garlic. Add the tomato and the parsley or coriander. Cover and cook for a further 5 minutes.

Serve with salad.

Kebab-e-dip-e-Uzbeki

Uzbeki kebab dip

For 2¼ lb (1 kg) minced meat

3 medium-sized onions
2 tomatoes
1 sweet pepper (or 3 hot peppers)
4 cloves garlic
Watercress, according to taste
2 tbsp (30 ml) vinegar
1½ tsp salt
1 tsp sugar
Juice of ½ lemon

Place all the vegetables in a liquidiser and blend.
   Mix in the vinegar, salt and sugar. Then add the lemon juice and leave to one side for 10 minutes before use.

Rhub-e-kebab

Kebab sauce

Makes 2 pints (1 l)

2 lb (900 g) tomatoes
1 bunch fresh coriander
2 medium onions
1 whole garlic bulb
3 green chillies
3 whole walnuts (optional)
6 tbsp vinegar
4 tbsp water
Juice of 1 lemon
½ tsp ground cumin
2 tsp salt
1½ tsp sugar

Peel the tomatoes, liquidise and put into a large bowl.

Liquidise the coriander, onions, garlic, green chillies and walnuts (optional). Add to the tomatoes, together with the vinegar, water, lemon juice, cumin, salt and sugar.

Bottle the sauce, which will keep for up to 3 months in the refrigerator.

Brinj Rice dishes

Chalau Steamed long-grain rice

Chalau-e-laidam Chalau with spinach

Mast chalau Chalau with yoghurt

Shibet chalau Chalau with dill

Pelau (i) Spiced, coloured long-grain rice

Pelau (ii) Pelau with chicken

Norange pelau Orange pelau with sweet rice

Sabzi pelau Spinach pelau

Norange pelau-e-do dama Orange pelau,
steamed twice

Yakhni pelau Savoury pelau

Kabeli Pelau with raisins, nuts and carrots

Uzbeki kabeli

Bata Short-grain rice

Kechree qorout Bata with meatballs and yoghurt

Mastawa Bata with lamb, chickpeas and herbs

Shola-e-gushti   Bata with mung beans

Shola-e-ghorbanda   Curry with bata and beans

Dam pokht-e-tarkori   Bata with mixed vegetables

Brinj

Rice and meat form the basis of most Afghan meals. Rice may be served as *chalau, pelau, kabeli* or *bata*.

Chalau is the name for plain, steamed, long-grain white rice. Basmati is the best rice of this kind. It is usually served with *qorma*, for example *qorma sabzi*, and the dish then takes the name of the *qorma*, for example *sabzi chalau*.

Pelau is chalau rice to which other ingredients, mainly spices, are added before steaming. It is coloured and flavoured in this way.

Kabeli is *pelau* with specially prepared carrots and raisins added. It is named after the capital of Afghanistan, Kabul. No festive occasion or party is complete without *kabeli*.

Bata is short-grain rice. Sometimes it is served with *qorma*, for example *shalgam qorma* and the dish takes the name of the *qorma*, for example *shalgam bata*. However, there are a number of short-grain rice dishes which are a substantial meal in themselves or can form one of many dishes for a party or festive meals.

How to cook chalau rice

For best results, soak the rice for ½–1 hour before using.

Step A
Using a saucepan large enough to take 4½ lb (2 kg) rice, boil 4 pts (2 litres) of water. Drain the uncooked rice and add to the boiling water. Boil for about 2½ minutes, until the rice is softish, but not more than 3 minutes. Drain, and rinse with two cups of cold water. Drain well.

Step B
Put the semi-cooked rice in the saucepan, taking care to avoid breaking the grains. Measure the stock which you have left aside (the nature of this stock will depend on individual rice dishes). It should be 1 pint. If less, make it up with a little hot water. Mix slowly until rice is thoroughly coloured with stock.

Step C (Steaming)
Very gently pile up the rice. Make a small hole through to the bottom of the rice with a long wooden-spoon handle. Make 4 similar holes, including one in the centre of the mixture. These holes allow the steam to disperse throughout the rice. If you are using meat, place it in the middle of the rice and pile rice on top.

Step D
Place a clean tea-towel on the underside of the saucepan lid, securing it with a knot on top of the lid before placing it firmly on the pan. Put a weight on top of the lid to keep the steam from escaping.

Leave on a high heat for 5 minutes and then cook for 25 minutes on a low heat.

Spices and colouring for pelau rice

The presentation of dishes is very important in Afghanistan, hence the spicing and colouring for *pelau*. This is prepared from caramel, dried onion, fresh onion, tomato or saffron. The following methods should make enough for 2 lb (1 kg) rice.

Caramel
2 tbsp oil
2 tbsp white sugar
½ pint (280 ml) chicken stock

Heat the oil in a small saucepan until it is very hot. Add the sugar and continue to heat until it caramelises, gently turning the saucepan to distribute the caramel through the oil. Half fill your kitchen sink with cold water and gently lower the base of the saucepan into it, taking care to keep your body well away in case the mixture sizzles and spits. When the caramel has cooled, add the stock and boil for 5 minutes. The caramel keeps 1–2 months if stored in a cool place.

Onion
8 oz (225 g) onion, finely sliced
6 tbsp (90 ml) oil

Fry the onion in the oil until golden-brown. Remove from the oil and allow to cool on a plate lined with kitchen paper. The onion will become crisp. Purée, and the colouring is ready for use.

Onion and tomato purée

4 oz (110 g) onion, finely sliced
1 tbsp tomato purée
6 tbsp (90 ml) corn oil
1 pint (550 ml) stock or water

Fry the onion in the oil until golden-brown. Separate the fried onion from the oil and drain on kitchen paper. Leave it to cool.

Add 1 tbsp of tomato purée to the oil and fry for 2 minutes. Add the water or stock and boil for 2 more minutes. The colouring is then ready for use.

Saffron and tomato

For colouring 2–3 lbs (1–1·3 kg) rice
½ lb (225 g) fresh tomatoes, peeled
¼ tsp saffron powder
½ cup (90 ml) corn oil
½ pint (280 ml) water or stock

Dissolve the saffron in half the stock or water. Place to one side.

Peel and chop the tomatoes finely. Fry in hot oil until the juice has evaporated and the colour has turned to dark red. Add the rest of the stock or water and the saffron and boil for 2 minutes. The colouring is now ready for use.

Chalau

Steamed long-grain rice

Serves 4   Preparation time: 45 minutes

1 lb (450 g) basmati rice
2 pints (1 l) water
½ pint (280 ml) stock
4 tbsp (60 ml) corn oil
1½ tsp salt
1 tsp cumin seeds (optional)

Wash the rice thoroughly in lukewarm water until the water runs clear. Then soak it in cold water for ½–1 hour, with ½ tsp salt.

Boil 2 pints of water and 1 tsp oil in a large saucepan.

Drain the rice and add it to the boiling water. Boil for 2½ minutes only. Drain, and then rinse with cold water, taking care to avoid breaking the rice. Drain well.

In a small saucepan boil the stock, oil, salt and cumin seeds (optional) for 1 minute.

Pour the rice and prepared liquid into a heavy-based saucepan. Mix well together. The saucepan used should be large enough to take two and a half times the volume of uncooked rice. Then follow the instructions on p. 132 from step C.

Serve *chalau* piled high on an oval dish. It is best eaten with any kind of *qorma* and salad.

Chalau-e-laidam

Chalau with spinach

Serves 4   Preparation time: 1¼ hours

2 lb (900 g) basmati rice
2½ pints (1·5 l) water
1 tsp oil
12 tbsp (180 ml) corn oil or olive oil
8 oz (225 g) onions, peeled and finely chopped
1 bunch spring onions
2 cloves garlic, peeled and finely chopped
½ tsp fresh ginger, peeled and finely chopped or
    grated
1–2 green chillies, de-seeded and finely chopped
4 oz (110 g) coriander, washed thoroughly and
    finely chopped
12 oz (340 g) spinach, puréed or finely chopped
½ tbsp salt
½ pint (280 ml) water
Juice of ½ lemon

Wash the rice thoroughly in lukewarm water until
the water runs clear, then soak it in cold water
while you prepare the spinach.

Heat the oil in a large, heavy-based saucepan
and sauté the onions over a medium flame until
soft. Add the spring onions, garlic, ginger and
green chilli. Cook until slightly golden, stirring
from time to time. Add the coriander and cook for
2 minutes.

Reduce heat to low. Add the spinach and cook for a further 5 minutes. Add the salt and mix well. Continue to cook until the vegetables are soft and integrated. The water should have evaporated and the oil separated out.

Add the water and lemon juice. Cook for 2 minutes and then leave to one side

Follow the method described on p. 132 for cooking the rice. When you steam the rice, pile it up with layers of spinach mixture and cook slowly for 30 minutes, keeping the saucepan well covered.

Serve *chalau laidam* piled high on a large oval dish.

Mast chalau

Chalau with yoghurt

Serves 4   Preparation time: 45 minutes

Cook your rice, following the method for *chalau* on p. 132.

When serving, top the *chalau* with 1 tbsp natural yoghurt and sprinkle with granulated sugar or honey.

Shibet chalau

Chalau with dill

Serves 4   Preparation time: 45 minutes

In Afghanistan, almost every family has either fresh or dried dill at their disposal. It is considered a good aid to digestion.

Cook as for *chalau* (p. 132) substituting stock for water and adding 1 tbsp dried or fresh dill.

Dill *chalau* goes well with a kebab dish.

Pelau (i)

Spiced, coloured long-grain rice

Serves 4   Preparation time: 1 hour

There are many forms of *pelau*, some more simple than others. The basis is always the same: steam-cooking rice, with the addition of natural colours and spices. You can vary your choice of spices and natural colouring.

1 lb (450 g) basmati rice
1 tsp salt
1 tsp black pepper
1 tsp cardamom powder
½ tbsp ground cumin
½ tsp *pelau masala* (p. xv)
6 tbsp (90 ml) vegetable oil
½ pint (280 ml) caramel colouring (p. 133)
2 pints (1 l) water for boiling rice

Prepare the rice following step A on p. 132.

Heat the caramel colouring. Add half the oil, the spices and seasonings. Mix well and leave to one side. Then add to rice when it is ready for steaming (see p. 132).

After steaming, heat the remaining oil and spoon through the *pelau*.

Serve heaped up on a large oval dish.

Pelau (ii)

Pelau with chicken

Serves 4   Preparation time: 1 hour 30 minutes

1 lb (450 g) basmati rice
6 tbsp (90 ml) corn or vegetable oil
1 lb (450 g) chicken or other meat cut into 2-inch
  cubes
½ lb (225 g) onion, peeled and finely sliced
2 pints (1 l) water
1 tsp salt
⅛ tsp turmeric
⅛ tsp chilli powder
½ tsp *pelau masala* (p. xv)
½ chicken stock cube
½ freshly ground cardamom
½ tsp dried coriander
½ tsp cumin
½ tsp black pepper

Prepare the rice, following step A on p. 132.

Heat the oil in a large heavy-based saucepan and
fry the onions until golden-brown. Reserving the
oil, remove the onions and spread them on a plate
lined with kitchen paper to cool and become crisp.
Purée and set to one side.

Measure the oil and make up to 6 tbsp again.
Fry the chicken (or other meat) over a high flame
for 5 minutes. Remove from the oil.

Measure the oil and make up to 3 tbsp. Heat and

add the chicken or meat, 1 pint water and salt. Bring to the boil. Cover, and cook over a medium flame for 15 minutes.

Add the turmeric and chilli powder. Continue to cook over medium heat for 5 minutes. Add the onion purée and stir in well. Add ½ pint water. Bring to the boil. The chicken should now be tender, but if you are using other meat, continue to cook it until it is tender – the time it takes will depend on the cut of meat used. Add the *pelau masala*.

Remove chicken or meat. Crumble the chicken stock cube into the liquid. Leave aside. You should have ¾ pint (425 ml) stock.

Follow the instructions for cooking rice step B on p. 132. Remember that your saucepan should be large enough to take two and a half times the volume of uncooked rice.

After mixing in the stock, add the cumin and coriander. Stir through gently so that the whole mixture becomes coloured. Then follow the instructions for steaming rice (steps C and D, p. 132).

Serve on a large oval dish. *Pelau* is always served with salad and *qorma*.

Norange pelau

Orange pelau with sweet rice

Serves 8   Preparation time: 2 hours

This is a main course and dessert prepared for festive occasions or weddings. A sweet orange rice, *zarda*, can be served as a dessert. A little of it is used to decorate the orange *pelau*.

For the zarda
2 oranges (Seville oranges may be used when they
    are in season)
Water
2 tbsp granulated sugar
5 oz (135 g) almonds, finely chopped
1½ oz (35 g) pistachio nuts, finely chopped
¼ tsp saffron
Corn or vegetable oil
15 cardamoms, 5 whole and 10 freshly ground
½ tsp ground cardamom
1 lb (450 g) rice

Slice off the stalk ends of the oranges and cut them vertically into quarters. Carefully peel off the skin. Discard the pith and cut the peel into long thin strips. Place the orange peel in a small pan and cover with water. Bring to the boil and drain. Repeat the process once for sweet oranges and twice for Seville oranges.

Dissolve the sugar in ½ pint water. Add the

143

orange peel, almonds, pistachio nuts, saffron and cardamom. Bring to the boil and simmer for 3 minutes.

Boil 2 pints (1 l) water. Add 1 lb (450 g) rice. Boil for 1 minute, keeping covered. Drain well. Put the rice in a saucepan. Add orange peel mixture and the saffron dissolved in 2½ fl oz (60 ml) boiling water and 2 tbsp oil. Mix gently. Pile high into a rounded pyramid in a very large saucepan. Sprinkle with ½ tsp ground cardamom. Steam in the normal way (see p. 132) for 30 minutes. After cooking, *zarda* is ready to eat as a sweet dish or a garnish for orange *pelau*.

For the pelau
10½ oz (300 g) finely sliced onion
2 lb (900 g) chicken, shoulder or leg of lamb
  washed and cut into 3-inch cubes
1 pt (550 ml) stock
1 lb (450 g) rice
½ tsp ground cardamom
½ tbsp ground cumin
½ tbsp ground coriander
2 tsp salt
¼ pint (140 ml) corn or vegetable oil

Heat half the oil and sauté the onions until they are golden-brown. Remove from the pan and spread on a plate lined with kitchen paper to cool and crispen. Purée and leave to one side.

Measure the oil and make it up to 6 tbsp. Sauté the meat until golden. Add the stock and bring to the boil. Add the onion purée. Cover and simmer gently until the meat is tender. Then top up the meat juices with water to measure ½ pint (280 ml).

Prepare the rice by following step A on p. 132, adding a pinch of saffron powder.

Take a large saucepan, and stir ½ pint (280 ml)

meat stock with the rice. Mix in the cumin, coriander and cardamom gently. Place the meat in the middle of the rice and pile the rest on top. Follow steps C and D for steaming rice on p. 132.

Put the meat on a warmed large oval meat dish. Pile the *pelau* on top and garnish with some of the *zarda*, using the remainder as a dessert.

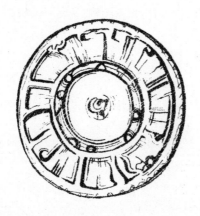

Sabzi pelau

Spinach pelau

Serves 4   Preparation time: 2 hours

2 lb (900 g) basmati rice
1 lb (450 g) spinach, fresh or frozen. If using
    frozen, gently thaw and allow water to
    evaporate
Small bunch coriander
1 large onion
½ pint (280 ml) oil
1½ lb (680 g) leg of lamb, cut into 1½-inch cubes
2 cloves garlic
2½ pints (1·5 l) water
2 medium tomatoes
2 tsp salt
½ tsp black pepper
1 stock cube (preferably lamb)
1 tbsp dried dill *or* ¼ tbsp fresh dill
Juice of 1 lemon
1 tsp *pelau masala* (p. xv)

Soak and rinse the rice.

Wash the spinach thoroughly. Remove tough
stalks and shake off excess water. Wash the coriander thoroughly. Finely chop spinach and coriander
in food processor. Leave to one side.

Finely chop the onion. Fry in 12 tbsp oil until
light golden. Add the meat and chopped garlic and

146

lightly brown. Add ½ pint (280 ml) water and cook until the water is evaporated.

Add the skinned and sliced tomatoes. Cook until the tomatoes soften. Add the spinach, salt, pepper, coriander and dill and fry for 5 minutes on low heat.

Dissolve the stock cube in 1½ (850 ml) pints water. Add to the meat, cover, and simmer until the meat is tender and the oil has separated out, stirring from time to time. Add the lemon juice and the rest of the water. Leave to one side.

Follow step A for cooking rice (p. 132).

Take a large saucepan; remembering that for steaming rice the saucepan should be large enough to take two and a half times the volume of uncooked rice. Spoon in half the rice, then the meat. Spoon in the remainder of the rice over the top. Gently fold in the remainder of the vegetable mixture ensuring the meat does not shift position. Add the *pelau masala*.

Follow steps C and D on p. 132 for steaming rice.

Before serving, spoon the excess oil from the frying pan gently through the *pelau*.

Serve *sabzi pelau* piled high on an oval dish.

Norange pelau-e-do dama

Orange pelau, steamed twice

Serves 4–6   *Preparation time: 1 hour 30 minutes*

This dish is made on very special occasions like weddings. Cooking orange *pelau* has its special needs. Two saucepans large enough to hold 4 lbs (2 kgs) of rice are needed.

For the topping
8 oz (225 g) sugar
Peel of 3 oranges
3½ oz (100 g) almonds, soaked in hot water, peeled and cut into quarters
15 whole cardamom pods
½ tsp saffron, dissolved in ¼ pint (140 ml) hot water
3½ oz (100 g) pistachio nuts, soaked in hot water, peeled and cut in half

Peel the oranges carefully. Discard the pith and cut the peel into thin strips. Put in water and bring to boiling point. Repeat the process twice and strain, reserving the coloured water.

Dissolve the sugar in 1½ pints (850 ml) water. Boil until the syrup is reduced to about 1 pint, after approximately 15 minutes. Boil the orange strips, saffron, almonds, pistachios, and cardamom seeds in the syrup for 1 minute.

For the pelau
2 lb (900 g) Tilda basmati rice
12 tbsp (180 ml) oil
10½ oz (300 g) chopped onion
2 lb (900 g) lamb, beef or chicken
2 tsp salt
½ tbsp green cardamom, freshly ground

Wash and soak the rice for ½–1 hour before cooking.

Fry the onion until light golden-brown and purée.

Cut the meat into 3-inch cubes. Using the oil from the fried onion, fry the meat for 15 minutes, until light golden-brown. Add 2 pints (1 l) water, the onion purée and salt. Cover the saucepan and cook for 20 minutes on a medium heat until the meat is tender, but make sure that the sauce is not reduced to less than ¾ pint. Add hot water if necessary.

Boil 3½ pints (2 l) water. Drain the rice and boil for 2 minutes. Drain, rinse with 1 pint cold water and drain again very well.

Place the rice in one of the saucepans taking care not to break the grains. Now add the sauce and mix in gently until the rice is evenly coloured.

Pile the rice up high in the saucepan and make holes through with the handle of a wooden spoon.

Steam the *pelau* for 15 minutes, in the usual way (p. 132).

Remove half the rice and put it in the second saucepan with the meat in the middle. Pour ½ pint (280 ml) syrup over it.

Pile the rest of the rice on top, with the rest of the syrup, spices, nuts and orange peel strips. Sprinkle with cardamom powder and steam for another 30 minutes.

To serve, remove the nuts and orange strips and use for decoration.

Yakhni pelau

Savoury pelau

Serves 6–8   *Preparation time: 1 hour*

2 lb (900 g) basmati rice
1 lb (450 g) onions, peeled and finely sliced
12 tbsp (180 ml) oil
2 lb (900 g) lamb or chicken
½ tsp tumeric
2 tsp salt
6 pints (3·5 l) water
1 tsp cardamom seeds
½ tsp cinnamon
½ black cardamom
3 cloves
½ tsp black pepper
1 lamb stock cube
½ tsp saffron

Heat the oil. Add the onions and fry until brown. Remove from oil. Spread on kitchen paper, leave to cool and then purée.

Cut the meat into 6 or 8 portions and fry until light golden-brown. Add 1 pint (550 ml) water and cook the meat until tender. Add the onion paste, salt, turmeric and stock cube. Boil for 5 minutes and leave to one side.

Follow steps A and B on p. 132 for cooking rice, except that 5 pints (3 l) water should be used and approximately ¾ pint (425 ml) stock. Then steam the rice in the usual way (see p. 132), with the meat well covered.

Pour 2 tbsp of oil over rice 1 minute before serving (this is optional). A popular accompaniment to *Yakhni pelau* is *muraba-e-alobolow* cherry jam (p. 238) or pickles.

Kabeli

Pelau with nuts, carrots and raisins

Serves 6–8   *Preparation time: 1 hour 30 minutes*

4 oz (110 g) almonds
4 oz (110 g) pistachios
2 lb (900 g) basmati rice
2 lb (900 g) lamb or boiling fowl
3 large carrots
1 lb (450 g) onion, finely sliced vertically
8 seedless raisins
12 tbsp (180 ml) oil
1½ pints (850 ml) warm water
½ tbsp tomato purée
1 chicken stock cube
1 tbsp ground cumin
1 tbsp ground coriander
1 tsp ground black pepper
½ tbsp ground green cardamom
⅛ tsp ground black cardamom
¼ tsp cinnamon
⅛ tsp ground cloves
2 tsp salt

Soak the almonds and pistachios in hot water, peel and cut them into halves and place in cold water.

Wash the rice thoroughly in lukewarm water until the water runs clear. Soak the rice for 30 minutes before cooking.

Cut the lamb or chicken into 8 pieces (approx. 3 inches square).

Cut carrots into long, thin strips and lightly cook in 3 tbsp oil, for 2–3 minutes. Add raisins, almonds and pistachios and cook for a further 2 minutes on a low heat. Set aside.

Fry half the onion in half the oil until golden-brown, or for about 4–5 minutes. Remove the onion and leave it to crispen. Then purée.

Place the remaining oil and onion into the pan in which the first onion was fried and fry till light golden-brown. Add the meat or chicken and fry for 3–4 minutes. Add ½ pint water and 2 tsp salt. Bring to the boil and cook until the water completely evaporates. Add the tomato purée and fry for 3 more minutes. Add 1 pint water and the chicken stock cube and leave on a medium heat until the meat is tender.

Separate the meat from the sauce and leave aside. Mix the onion purée with the sauce, boil for 1 minute and keep to one side.

Follow steps A and B on p. 132 to cook the rice. Sprinkle the ground cumin, coriander, black pepper, green cardamom, black cardamom, cinnamon and cloves over the rice. Place the almonds, raisins and pistachios in the middle and cover with rice, piling it up high. Arrange the meat around the edge and make holes through the rice pile with the handle of a wooden spoon.

Follow step D on p. 132 for steaming the rice.

Take the meat out carefully, and keep it in a separate dish. Then gently take out the almonds, raisins, pistachios and carrots. Put the meat on a large serving dish and cover with the rice. Top with the almonds, raisins, pistachios and carrots for decoration.

Uzbeki kabeli

Serves 12   Preparation time: 1 hour

2 lb (900 g) basmati rice
½ lb (225 g) raisins
1½ lb (700 g) mutton or lamb, cut into large pieces
  about 4 inches square
2 tsp salt
12 tbsp (180 ml) corn oil
1 lb (450 g) onions, peeled and cut into circles
  approximately ⅜ inch thick
1 lb (450 g) carrots scraped and cut into long thin
  strips approximately 3 inches long
1 tsp tomato purée
10 whole cardamoms
1 chicken stock cube
1 tbsp black pepper
1 tbsp ground cumin
½ tsp *pelau masala* (p. xv)

Wash the rice in cold water until the water runs
clear. Wash the raisins and leave to soak with the
rice in cold water for five minutes.

Wash the meat, drain and leave to dry.

Heat the oil in a very large, heavy saucepan.
Sauté the meat over a high flame until the water
has evaporated (approximately 10 minutes). Add
the onions and stir. Continue to fry over a medium
heat, stirring from time to time. After 5 minutes
add 2 tsp salt and ½ pint water. Continue to fry.
After 10 minutes the meat and onions should be
brown. Add the tomato purée and continue to fry

for 2 more minutes. Add 2 pints water and bring to the boil. Cover and simmer until meat is tender. Add the carrots, cover the saucepan and leave gently cooking for 15 minutes. Add the cardamom.

Dissolve the stock cubes in 1 pint (550 ml) boiling water. Add the raisins and rice and boil for 10 minutes over a high heat. Add the cumin, black pepper and *pelau masala* and cook over a medium heat. When the water has almost all evaporated, lower the heat and steam in the usual way (p. 132) for 30 minutes. Pour in the meat juices with the meat.

Serve piled high on a large oval dish.

Bata

Short-grain rice

Serves 8   Preparation time: 45 minutes

1 lb (450 g) short-grain rice
3 pints (1·75 l) water
2 chicken or beef stock cubes
3 tbsp (45 ml) vegetable oil
1 tsp salt

Wash the rice until the water runs clear and drain well.

Boil the water and add the stock cubes, rice, oil and salt. Bring back to the boil and simmer over a low heat until nearly all the water is absorbed.

Cover the lid with a cloth, place back on the saucepan and use a weight to keep the lid on firmly. Continue to cook over a very low flame until all the water is absorbed (approximately 30 minutes).

Serve with aubergine *qorma* (p. 65) or spinach *qorma* (p. 77).

Kechree qorout

Bata with meatballs and yoghurt

Serves 8   Preparation time: 2 hours

For the meatballs
1 lb (450 g) finely minced beef or lamb
1 medium onion, finely chopped
1 tsp salt
½ tsp freshly ground black pepper
1 tbsp dried coriander
1 tbsp fresh coriander, finely chopped
3 cloves garlic (crushed)
1 tsp fresh/dry ginger
½ pint (280 ml) tomato juice

Combine all the meatball ingredients together and mix very well. Shape into balls the size of hazelnuts and cook as for *kofta* (p. 47).

10½ oz (300 g) whole mung beans, soaked overnight
3½ pints (2 l) water
1 chicken stock cube
1 lb (450 g) short-grain rice
1 tsp salt
1 tsp freshly ground black pepper
¼ tsp turmeric
½ pint (280 ml) tomato juice
12 tbsp (180 ml) corn or vegetable oil
2 tsp dill

1 carton strained yoghurt or Greek-style yoghurt
Fresh coriander and dried mint to garnish

Wash the beans and drain. Boil them in the water
and dissolved stock cube, cover and simmer for 15
minutes or until the beans are beginning to soften.

Add the well-washed and drained rice, stock and
remaining ingredients except meatballs, yoghurt
and dried mint. Bring to the boil and simmer until
most of the liquid is absorbed, but the rice is still
firm. Cover and steam (step D, p. 132) for about
30 minutes.

Serve piled high on a large oval meat dish, decor-
ated with the meatballs and with a bowl of yoghurt
in the centre. Garnish with finely chopped fresh
coriander and dried mint.

Mastawa

Bata with lamb, chickpeas and herbs

Serves 8   *Preparation time: 2 hours (and time for soaking)*

4 oz (110 g) chickpeas
2 oz (50 g) orange peel strips about 1¼ inches long
1½ lb (700 g) short-grain rice
⅛ tsp saffron
12 tbsp (180 ml) oil
1 medium onion, finely sliced
2½ lb (1·14 kg) lamb – leg or shoulder – cut into 2-inch squares
4 large cloves garlic, crushed
1½ tsp salt
1 tsp chilli powder
1 pint (550 ml) stock
1 packet vegetable soup to make 1½ pints (850 ml) soup
Juice of 1 lemon
½ tsp dried mint
½ tsp dried dill
1 tbsp fresh dill
16 oz (450 g) natural low fat yoghurt
10 oz (280 g) soured cream
1 tbsp freshly ground black pepper

Soak the chickpeas in hot water for 2 hours. Drain

159

and cook in fresh water until soft. Strain and leave to one side.

Cut long, thin strips of orange peel, ensuring that all the pith is removed. Cover with water and leave to soak for 1 hour.

Wash the rice thoroughly in lukewarm water until the water runs clear, then soak it in cold water for 1–2 hours.

Cover the saffron with 3 tbsp boiling water and leave to soak.

Heat 10 tbsp oil in a large heavy-based saucepan. Sauté the onions until light brown. Dry them on kitchen paper and then purée. Leave to one side.

Fry the meat in the same oil until light golden in colour. Add the garlic, salt, chilli powder and puréed onion. Make up the packet soup and add it to the meat. Bring to the boil and simmer until the meat is tender. Remove the meat and bone it.

Measure the liquid and make it up to 1 pint (550 ml) with boiling water. Place in a very large saucepan. Drain the rice and add it to the liquid. Bring to the boil and boil rapidly for 7 minutes, adding a further 1 pint (550 ml) boiling water if water evaporates. Add the meat, chickpeas and lemon juice.

Heat 2 tbsp oil, add the dried mint and dried dill and simmer for about 30 seconds. Add to the meat and rice mixture. Add the fresh dill, orange peel and saffron. Mix the ingredients well but gently.

Cover the saucepan and steam for 35 minutes (step D, p. 132). Take saucepan off the heat and gently fold the soured cream and yoghurt into the rice. Sprinkle with black pepper.

Serve with onion salad, green chillies and bread.

Shola-e-gushti

Bata with mung beans

Serves 6–8   Preparation time: 2 hours

12 tbsp (180 ml) corn or vegetable oil
2 medium onions, peeled and finely chopped
2 lb (900 g) leg of lamb, cut into 4-inch pieces
1 tsp salt
¼ tsp turmeric
½ pint (280 ml) tomato juice
1½ pints (850 ml) water
1 lb 2 oz (500 g) short-grain rice
10½ oz (300 g) split mung dal green beans, soaked
  overnight
2 tsp freshly ground black pepper
4 pints (2·25 l) water *or* 2 pints (1 l) stock and 1
  chicken stock cube dissolved in 2 pints (1 l) water
1 tsp *pelau masala* (p. xv)
1 tsp chilli powder
2 tsp dill
1 tsp ground coriander

Sauté the onions until light golden-brown. Add
the meat and salt and fry for 5 minutes. Add the
turmeric and ½ pint (280 ml) water. Bring to the
boil and simmer until the water evaporates and the
oil separates out. Fry the meat mixture for a further
5 minutes. Add the tomato juice. Bring to the boil
and simmer until the water evaporates and the
oil separates out. Continue to cook, stirring for 2

minutes. Add 1 pint (550 ml) water. Cover, and simmer until the meat is tender.

Wash the rice and split green beans. Add 4 pints (2·25 l) water or stock and water to the meat mixture. Add the rice and beans and all remaining ingredients and simmer over a low heat until nearly all the water is absorbed.

Cover and steam following step D, p. 132.

Pile high on a large oval meat dish and serve with yoghurt salad.

Shola-e-ghorbanda

Curry with bata and beans

Serves 6–8   Preparation time: 2 hours

For the qorma (curry)
6 tbsp (90 ml) corn or vegetable oil
1 lb (450 g) onions, peeled, chopped finely
1 lb (450 g) leg of lamb on the bone cut into 1½-
    inch cubes
2 cloves garlic, peeled and crushed
1 tsp fresh ginger, grated
3 green chillies, chopped
1 tsp salt
¼ tsp turmeric
1 pint (550 ml) water *or* ¾ pint (425 ml) water and
    ¼ pint (140 ml) stock
¼ tsp fresh coriander, finely chopped
½ tsp cardamom powder
Juice of 1 small lemon

Heat the oil in a large, heavy-based saucepan and
sauté the onions for about 5 minutes over a high
flame until light golden-brown.

Add the meat and sauté over a high flame until
light golden-brown, adding the garlic, ginger, chillies and salt after 5 minutes. Sauté for a further 2
minutes. Add ½ pint (280 ml) water and cook for
a further 10 minutes. Add the turmeric and ½ pint
(280 ml) water. Cover, and simmer until the meat
is tender.

Remove the lid and fry the *qorma* over a low

163

flame for 3 minutes, adding the black pepper. Add the stock and cardamom powder and leave on a low flame until ready to serve.

Sprinkle the coriander and lemon juice over the *qorma*.

For the shola-e-gorbanda
2 medium onions, peeled and finely chopped
⅛ tsp turmeric
½ pint (280 ml) tomato juice
10½ oz (300 g) whole mung beans, soaked overnight
1 lb (450 g) short-grain rice, well washed and drained
1 tsp salt
2 tsp freshly ground black pepper
12 tbsp (180 ml) corn or vegetable oil
4 pints (2.25 l) water and 1 chicken stock cube
2 tsp *pelau masala* (p. xv)
1 tsp chilli powder
1 tsp ground dried coriander
Finely chopped fresh coriander to garnish

Sauté the onions until golden. Add the turmeric and continue to cook for 30 seconds. Add the tomato juice, the water (4 pints) and stir, adding the stock cube. Bring to the boil. Add the mung beans and cover. Continue to cook until the beans begin to soften – about 15 minutes. Add the rice and remaining ingredients. Bring to the boil then simmer over a low heat until almost all the water is absorbed.

Steam by the method described in steps C and D on p. 132.

Place the *qorma* in the centre of a large oval dish and pile the rice and beans around it. Garnish with the coriander and serve.

Dam pokht-e-tarkori

Bata with mixed vegetables

Serves 4   Preparation time: 1 hour 30 minutes

6 tbsp (90 ml) oil
1 medium onion
1 lb (450 g) meat on the bone, cut into small pieces
2 small tomatoes
2 small carrots
Few leaves spinach
1½ tsp salt
1 green chilli
Few sprigs fresh coriander, chopped
1 lb (450 g) rice
Pinch saffron powder
½ tsp cumin powder
½ tsp black pepper powder
½ tsp cardamom powder
Water

Sauté the onion for about 5 minutes until deep golden-brown. Add the meat, tomatoes, carrots and spinach. Fry for 5 minutes.

Add ½ pint (280 ml) water, salt, green chilli and coriander. Boil until the meat is tender for 20 minutes. See that the stock made is not less than 2 pints (1 l) in quantity; if it falls short then add more water.

Add the rice with the saffron, cumin and black pepper. Boil on medium heat until the rice is reasonably soft and the water has almost evaporated. Pile the rice up and sprinkle with cardamom powder. Steam for 30 minutes on a very low heat (see p. 132).

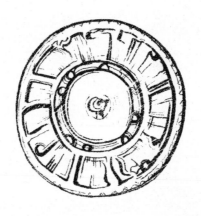

Tarkori Vegetables

Samarok lawang Mushrooms with sour cream

Sosani banjan Aubergine curry

Bouranee banjan Aubergine and peppers in yoghurt dressing

Sabzi palak (i) Spinach with tomatoes and onions

Sabzi palak (ii) Spinach with cream and leeks

Samarok lawang

Mushrooms with sour cream

Serves 6   Preparation time: 20 minutes

2 medium onions, finely chopped
4 tbsp (60 ml) corn oil
3 cloves garlic, finely chopped
1 tsp fresh ginger, grated
2 green chillies, de-seeded and finely chopped
1½ lb (700 g) button mushrooms, washed and
   dried
1 tsp salt
¼ tsp turmeric
½ pint (280 ml) hot water
5 oz (135 g) sour cream
A few parsley leaves for garnish

Sauté the onions until light golden-brown. Add
the garlic, ginger, chillies, mushrooms and salt and
fry gently for 10 minutes. Add the turmeric and
continue to cook for 2 minutes. Add the water,
cover and simmer until the mushrooms are soft.
Fold in the sour cream and garnish with parsley
leaves.

Serve with a meat *qorma* dish.

Sosani banjan

Aubergine curry

Serves 8   Preparation time: 30 minutes

2 lb (900 g) aubergines
9 tbsp (135 ml) corn, olive or vegetable oil
8 oz (225 g) onion, peeled and finely chopped
1 tbsp ginger, finely chopped
1 green chilli, de-seeded and finely chopped
¼ tsp turmeric
½ tsp black pepper (optional)
¼ tsp salt
1 tsp paprika
½ tsp dried coriander
5 oz (135 g) double cream
1 medium tomato, chopped, and 1 tbsp chopped
  coriander to garnish

Gas Mark 7/220°C/430°F

Pre-heat the oven.

Rub the aubergine with a little oil and put in the oven until the inside is soft and the skin is wrinkled. Peel, and mash the flesh.

Heat the oil in a large, heavy-based saucepan. Sauté the onions until soft over a medium flame. Add the ginger and chilli and cook until slightly golden, stirring from time to time. Add the aubergine and spices and continue to cook until the vegetables are well cooked and integrated. Reduce heat to low.

Just before serving, gently fold in the cream and heat through. Garnish with the tomato and coriander and serve hot.

Bouranee banjan

Aubergine and peppers in yoghurt dressing

Serves 6   Preparation time: 30 minutes

1 lb (450 g) aubergines
½ tsp salt
Corn or vegetable oil for frying
2 medium onions, cut into rings
1 green pepper, de-seeded and cut into rings
1 red pepper, de-seeded and cut into rings
3 large tomatoes, sliced
¼ tsp hot chilli powder
4 tbsp (60 ml) water
1 pint (550 ml) strained yoghurt
3 cloves garlic, crushed

Peel the aubergines, unless they are small, in which case the peel can be left on. Cut into rings ½ inch thick. Spread out in a colander and sprinkle liberally with salt. Leave for 15 minutes for the juices to drain. Dry well with kitchen paper.

Take a frying pan with a lid. Cover the bottom well with oil. Fry the aubergine rings a few at a time until lightly browned on each side. Lift on to a plate, and fry the remaining slices, adding more oil as required.

Fry the onion gently until transparent. Remove to another plate.

Place a layer of aubergine in the frying pan. On

172

top of this place some onion rings, pepper rings and tomato slices. Repeat, adding a sprinkle of salt and chilli powder between layers. Pour over any remaining oil from the fried aubergine and onion, and add the water. Cover and simmer gently on a very low heat for 20 minutes, until the aubergine is tender.

Combine the yoghurt and crushed garlic, spread half over the base of a serving dish. Arrange the vegetables on top, keeping the layers and ensuring that the aubergine slices remain whole. Leave some juices in the frying pan.

Pour the remaining yoghurt mixture and vegetable juices over the layered vegetables and serve.

Sabzi palak (i)

Spinach with tomatoes and onions

Serves 6   Preparation time: 30 minutes

½ pint (280 ml) corn or vegetable oil
1 medium onion, peeled and finely chopped
1 tsp fresh ginger, grated
3 cloves garlic, peeled and finely chopped
2 tomatoes, peeled *or* ¼ pint (140 ml) tomato juice
3 bunches spinach, washed well and finely
   chopped
1 bunch coriander, washed well and finely
   chopped
1 bunch spring onions, peeled and finely chopped
2 green chillies, de-seeded and finely chopped
1 tsp salt
1 tsp pepper
1 pint (550 ml) stock

Heat the oil in a large, heavy-based saucepan and
fry the onions until golden. Add the ginger, garlic
and tomatoes (or half the tomato juice). Fry for 3
minutes.

Add the spinach, coriander, spring onions,
green chillies, salt and pepper. Mix well. Add the
stock or remaining tomato juice and mix well.
Cover, and cook for a further 15 minutes over a
medium flame until the water has evaporated, and
the oil separates out.

Fry for a further 5 minutes, stirring from time to
time. Serve hot.

Sabzi palak (ii)

Spinach with cream and leeks

Serves 6   Preparation time: 30 minutes

½ pint (280 ml) corn or olive oil
8 oz (225 g) onions, peeled and finely chopped
6 oz (170 g) leeks, washed thoroughly and finely
   chopped
2 cloves garlic, peeled and finely chopped
½ tsp fresh ginger, peeled and finely chopped or
   grated
1–2 green chilli, de-seeded and finely chopped.
4 oz (110 g) coriander, washed thoroughly and
   finely chopped
12 oz (340 g) spinach, puréed or chopped finely
1 tsp salt
Juice of ½ lemon
5 oz (135 g) double cream (optional)

Heat half the oil in a large, heavy-based saucepan.
Sauté the onions until soft over a medium flame.

Add the leeks, garlic, ginger and green chilli.
Cook until slightly golden, stirring from time to
time. Add the coriander and cook for 2 minutes.

Reduce the flame to low. Add the remaining oil
and fry the spinach purée for 5 minutes. Add the
salt and mix well. Continue to cook until vegetables are well cooked and integrated. The water
should evaporate and the oil separate out.

Add the lemon juice. Cook for a further 2 minutes.

Fold in the cream, gently heat through and serve with *chalau* rice (p. 132).

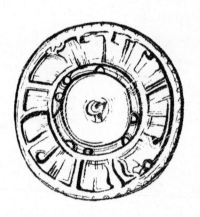

Sálate sabzijat Salads

Sálat ba kabeli Salad to accompany *kabeli*

Sálat maida (i) Mixed salad

Sálat maida (ii) Mixed salad

Sálat-e-muli safied Chinese radish salad

Sálat-e-piaz Onion salad

Sálat-e-mast Yoghurt salad

Sálat ba kabeli

Salad to accompany kabeli

Serves 6

¼ bunch fresh coriander
¼ cucumber
2 cloves garlic
3 tomatoes
1 bunch spring onions
Pinch of black pepper, salt, and dried mint
Juice of 1 lemon

Finely chop the coriander. Peel and finely chop the cucumber and add to the coriander with the crushed garlic. Peel and finely chop the tomatoes and spring onions and add together with the pepper, salt, mint and lemon juice.

Sálat maida (i)

Mixed salad

1 bunch spring onions
2 medium tomatoes
1 clove garlic
¼ cucumber
½ tsp salt
½ tsp pepper
Juice of ½ lemon
A few sprigs of fresh mint, finely chopped
½ bunch of coriander, finely chopped

Prepare the spring onions, discarding green part. Leave whole. Cut the tomatoes into small pieces and crush the garlic. Peel the cucumber and chop finely. Mix together, seasoning with salt and pepper.

Combine the lemon juice, mint and coriander and sprinkle on top.

Sálat maida (ii)

Mixed salad

1 head chinese leaf lettuce, washed well
¼ cucumber
Small onion, finely sliced
Pinch dried mint
2 small beetroots
Pinch of salt and pepper
1 tsp olive oil
1 apple, thinly sliced
1 small lemon

Shred lettuce into largish pieces. Toss in finely sliced cucumber.

Peel and finely slice onion, and apple and mix all ingredients together except onion. Garnish salad with the onion and a pinch of dried mint, and sprinkle with the lemon juice.

Sálat-e-muli safied

Chinese radish salad

2 lb (900 g) grated Chinese radish
1 crushed clove garlic
¼ tsp salt
4 heaped tbsp (60 g) low-fat natural yoghurt

Combine the radish, garlic and salt. Refrigerate for 5 minutes (or up to 4 hours if required, if covered with cling film).

Add the yoghurt just before serving.

Sálat-e-piaz

Onion salad

2 medium onions, peeled and finely chopped,
   marinated for 2 hours in lemon and salt
½ bunch coriander, washed and finely chopped
½ tsp salt
½ tsp pepper
Juice of ½ lemon
1 bunch pink radishes

Combine all the ingredients well and serve.

Sálat-e-mast

Yoghurt salad

1 small carton strained yoghurt
Juice of ½ lemon
2 cloves garlic, crushed
¼ cucumber, peeled and chopped
Pinch salt
Pinch dried mint
½ bunch spring onions, chopped finely

Mix all the ingredients together well.

Shernie Puddings and sweets

Abreshom kebab 'Silk' kebab

Afghan jelly

Vanilla and nut cake

Ferni Afghan custard

Loqema qazy Sweet egg balls

Molida Sweet wholemeal pudding

Shola shireen Rice pudding with nuts

Shir pera Milk and sugar sweets

Jelabi Sweet pancakes

Badam-e-shireen Sugared almonds

Badam-e-shour Salted almonds

Mast Afghan yoghurt

Haleem Oatmeal and chicken pudding

Qoymaq Sweet spicy dessert

Samanak Traditional wholemeal pudding

Faluda wa jhala Ice-cream and caramel dessert

Kishmish paneer Curd cheese with raisins

Semion Sweet noodles

Halwa-e-zardak Carrot halva

185

Abreshom kebab

'Silk' kebab

Serves 7

1 pint (550 ml) water
8 oz (225 g) castor sugar
4 tbsp honey
6 eggs
1 pt (550 ml) vegetable oil
7 tbsp (100 g) flaked almonds, roughly chopped
7 tbsp (100 g) pistachio nuts, chopped
1 tsp ground almonds
1 tsp ground pistachio nuts
1 tsp ground cardamom

Heat the water and dissolve the sugar and honey. Bring to the boil and cook until syrupy – approximately 15 minutes. Leave to one side.

Heat 1 inch oil in a large frying pan until very hot and bubbly, and then turn down to medium.

Meanwhile, beat the eggs with a fork or whisk until well beaten. Do not use a food processor or blender, as this produces too much froth.

Dip your fingers into the egg mixture and dribble a thin stream across the frying pan into the hot oil. Repeat this approximately 14 times, until the pan is nearly covered with a fine layer of egg mixture. The shape formed explains the name of this dish.

Cook until light golden-brown. Remove from the pan, letting excess oil drip back, and place flat on a plate. Sprinkle with 1 tbsp mixed chopped pistachio nuts and almonds. Roll up loosely, and sprinkle with a mixture of ground almonds, pistachio and cardamom.

Repeat this process six times, until all the mixture is used up. Pour syrup over each kebab, leave to cool and serve.

Afghan jelly

Serves 6

3 packets black cherry jelly
14 oz (400 g) tin crushed pineapple (or fresh if
  available)
14 oz (400 g) tin raspberries (or fresh if available)
4 tbsp (60 g) crushed almonds
4 tbsp (60 g) crushed walnuts
10 oz (280 g) whipping cream

Make up the jelly, using juice from the pineapple
and raspberries. Add water if necessary to make
approximately 2 pints.

Add 4 tbsp (60 ml) to the cream and whip until
thick. Add half the nuts and set to one side. This
is the topping.

Put the jelly in the refrigerator until it begins to
set, then stir in the pineapple and raspberries and
the rest of the chopped almonds and walnuts.
Leave to set.

Cover with topping and leave to set.

Vanilla and nut cake

Serves 6   Preparation time: 50 minutes

11 oz (300 g) butter
11 oz (300 g) icing sugar
6 large eggs
1 tsp vanilla essence
10 cardamom pods, finely ground
14 oz (400 g) sponge flour, sieved
2 oz (50 g) walnuts, finely chopped
2 oz (50 g) pistachios, finely chopped
2 oz (50 g) almonds, finely chopped

Gas Mark 7/220°C/430°F then Gas Mark
   6/205°C/400°F

Melt the butter, add the sugar and beat until thick
and creamy.
   Add the eggs and beat well.
   Add the vanilla essence and cardamom powder
and gradually add the sieved flour. Finally add
nuts.
   Grease a large cake tin (or 2 small tins) and line
with greaseproof paper.
   Pour in the cake mixture and bake in a pre-
heated oven at Gas Mark 7 for 20 minutes, then
Gas Mark 6 for 15 minutes.

Ferni

Afghan custard

Serves 3   Preparation time: 30 minutes

2 tbsp cornflour
1 pint (550 ml) milk
2 oz (50 g) castor sugar
¼ cup (60 ml) rosewater
⅓ tbsp ground cardamom
1 tbsp finely chopped pistachios

Mix the cornflour and sugar well with ¼ pint (140 ml) cold milk.

Bring the rest of the milk to the boil in a heavy-based saucepan. Add the cornflour and sugar mixture slowly, stirring all the time. Cook over a very low heat, continually stirring until the mixture reaches a consistency of thick cream.

Add the rosewater and half the ground cardamom. Stir well and cook for another minute.

Pour the *ferni* into individual glasses or on to an oval tray to cool. Put in the refrigerator to chill.

Sprinkle with remaining cardamom and pistachios and serve.

An alternative is yellow *ferni*, or carrot custard. Use the same ingredients, but add 2 small to medium-sized carrots, scraped and grated very finely. Follow the method for *ferni*, adding the carrots with ¼ pint (140 ml) water to the rest of the milk. Bring to the boil and continue as above.

191

Loqema qazy

Sweet egg balls

Serves 6   Preparation time: 30 minutes

6 oz (150 g) sugar
½ pint (280 ml) water
4 eggs
½ tsp bicarbonate of soda
9 oz (250 g) plain yoghurt
1 pint (550 ml) vegetable oil
Sesame seeds (optional)

Dissolve the sugar in the water and continue to cook until syrupy.

Beat the eggs until creamy. Add the bicarbonate of soda and yoghurt and continue to beat until well mixed.

Bring the oil to the temperature required for deep frying. Drop the mixture 1 tsp at a time into the hot oil and cook until light golden-brown. Remove from oil and coat with syrup.

Sprinkle with sesame seeds, if desired. Leave to cool on a plate.

Molida

Sweet wholemeal pudding

Serves 6   Preparation time: 40 minutes

In Afghanistan, *molida* is specially prepared for wedding feats. After the meal, the bride and groom sit on a couch covered with beautiful silks, traditionally from Benares, and set on a stage. In front of them is the wedding cake and the *molida*, piled high on a large oval plate. The bride gives a little *molida* on a spoon to the bridegroom and he in turn gives her the same. The plate is then passed around the guests and they each take and eat a spoonful of *molida*.

1½ lb (700 g) wholemeal flour
6 tbsp (90 ml) corn oil
1 tsp dried yeast
½ pint (280 ml) warm water – the temperature
    should not be higher than blood temperature
7 oz (200 g) castor sugar
2 tbsp ground cardamom
6 tbsp (90 ml) pure ghee (vegetable oil is not a
    suitable substitute here)

Gas Mark 7/220°C/430°F

Put the flour in a warm bowl. Add the oil, yeast and water. Knead well. Leave to rise for 30 minutes.

Divide the dough into five pieces. Very lightly oil 2–3 roasting pans and spread the dough in them. It should be about 1½ inches thick. Bake in the pre-heated oven until cooked – usually 15 minutes.

When cool, break the bread into pieces and grind in a food processor, with the ground cardamom, until it looks like fine breadcrumbs. Then mix in the sugar.

Heat the ghee and stir thoroughly through the mixture, making sure you keep the breadcrumb texture. Pile high on a plate and serve with ground cardamom sprinkled on top.

Shola shireen

Rice pudding with nuts

Serves 6   Preparation time: 1 hour 30 minutes

12 oz (340 g) pudding rice
2 pints (1 l) water
½ pint (280 ml) milk
½ tsp saffron strands dissolved in a little hot
   water for 1–2 hours
9 oz (250 g) sugar
1½ tbsp rosewater
4 oz (110 g) chopped pistachios and almonds
1 tbsp ground cardamom
1 tbsp ground pistachios
2 oz (50 g) butter

Wash the rice and soak for 30 minutes. Drain.

Bring the water to the boil. Add the rice and cook until soft. Add the sugar and when it is dissolved add the milk, butter, saffron and bring to the boil.

Add the rosewater and half the pistachios and almonds. Simmer for 10 minutes, stirring continuously.

When the water has been absorbed, cover the lid of the saucepan with a clean cloth and replace firmly on the saucepan. Leave on the lowest heat for 25 minutes.

Spread on an oval plate and garnish with the

ground cardamom and pistachio and the remaining chopped pistachios and almonds. Serve cold.

An alternative rice pudding is *shola-e-olba* rice pudding with *methi* seeds. Soak the seeds for 10 minutes, dry them lightly and then boil for another 3 minutes. Steam the rice for 30 minutes with the *methi* seeds, 9 oz (250 g) sugar and a pinch of saffron powder. Sprinkle with cardamom powder and serve hot. Use 4 tsp *methi* seeds to 1 lb (450 g) pudding rice.

Shir pera

Milk and sugar sweets

Serves 8   Preparation time: 30 minutes

This famous dish comes from the province of Hirat in western Afghanistan. The almonds and pistachios from the area are the best in the whole country. They give a special colour and flavour to *shir pera*, which is enjoyed on special occasions in many parts of Afghanistan.

2 lb (900 g) castor sugar
8 oz (225 g) powdered skimmed milk
6 oz (170 g) ground almonds
1 pint (550 ml) water
3 tbsp (45 ml) rosewater
2 tbsp ground cardamom
3 tbsp ground pistachio
1 tbsp butter

Boil the water and sugar in a medium-sized saucepan, until syrupy but not too thick.

Remove the saucepan from the stove. Add the powdered milk and butter and beat well into the syrup. Add the ground almonds and rosewater and mix well.

Oil a shallow square Pyrex dish thoroughly. Spread the mixture evenly across it. Sprinkle with the pistachio and cardamom.

While it is still warm, cut diagonal parallel lines

across the mixture to form diamond shapes. Leave to cool in the refrigerator.

Place in an airtight tin or rectangular plastic container, using greaseproof paper between the layers. Store in the refrigerator.

Jelabi

Sweet pancakes

Serves 6   Preparation time: 30 minutes

The amount of water used to prepare the batter affects the end product, so measure it accurately.

1 pint (550 ml) water
8 oz (225 g) sugar
2 tbsp golden syrup (optional)
10 oz (280 g) light self-raising flour
½ pint (280 ml) oil

Boil half the water. Add the sugar and boil until a slightly thick syrup is formed. Then add the golden syrup, mix well and leave in a warm place.

Mix the flour with the rest of the water to the consistency of thick cream. Pour into a plastic bottle with a small opening at top.

Heat some oil until very hot in a deep frying-pan. Starting from the middle or the outer edge of the pan, drip the batter in five rings to make a spiral pancake about the size of a saucer. Cook until the edges are light brown. After allowing any excess oil to drain away, remove the pancake. Repeat with the rest of the batter. Let each pancake cool separately for a few moments and then pile them on a plate and pour over the syrup.

Serve either with tea or as a sweet.

Badam-e-shireen

Sugared almonds

1 lb (450 g) peeled, whole, almonds
12 oz (340 g) castor sugar

Gas Mark 4/180°C/355°F

Heat the oven. Line a baking tray with greaseproof paper. Spread the almonds in roasting tin and place in the oven to heat up.

Melt the sugar in a medium-sized saucepan over a low heat, and gently heat until light brown. Add the warm almonds and mix thoroughly. Remove from the heat.

Spread very quickly in a single layer over the lined baking tray. Speed is essential, otherwise the mixture will harden, and will be impossible to spread. Allow to cool, then break into pieces and store in a tin or plastic container in a cool place. Leave the paper on until ready to eat.

Badam-e-shour

Salted almonds

1 lb (450 g) almonds, blanched
2 tbsp salt
3 tbsp water

Gas Mark 7/220°C/430°F

Heat the oven.

Mix the salt and water. Put the almonds and salted water into an oven dish and mix thoroughly. Put in the oven for 15 minutes, after which the almonds should be dry and crispy.

Store in a cool place in an airtight container.

Mast

Afghan yoghurt

2 pints (1 l) milk
2 oz (50 g) low fat live yoghurt

Heat the milk to just before boiling point, then allow to cool down.

Stir the yoghurt until it is smooth and add to the lukewarm milk, stirring continuously. Pour into a dish, cover with a cloth and keep in a warm place for 8 hours.

Haleem

Oatmeal and chicken pudding

Preparation time: 1 hour 30 minutes

Due to its nutritional properties, in that it keeps the body warm and invigorated, *haleem* is prepared during the winter months. Usually, *haleem* is eaten in the mornings.

1 lb 9 oz (700 g) fine oats
1 lb (450 g) chicken breasts
12 oz (340 g) pudding rice
2 tbsp salt
½ tbsp ground cinnamon
12 pints (6·25 l) water
9 oz (250 g) sugar or honey
2 tbsp ground cardamom
2 oz (50 g) almond, shelled and roughly chopped
2 oz (50 g) pistachio nuts, ground
6 tbsp (90 ml) corn oil

Wash and cut the chicken breasts into cubes. Boil in 1 pint (550 ml) water with 1 tsp salt for 15 minutes to tenderise. Then cut the softened cubes up further, and put back into the stock.

Next, wash the pudding rice and boil in 1 pint (550 ml) water and 1 tsp of salt until it is very soft and tender. Mix with the chicken and leave to one side.

Grind the oats in a food processor. It is important

that they are well ground, or they will take longer to cook and require more water when mashing. Boil the rest of the water and add the oats. Boil on a medium heat for 15 minutes. Now add the chicken and rice mixture and the rest of the salt. Continue to boil for 30 more minutes until the mixture is reasonably thick.

Add the cardamom and mix well. Now stir the mixture and turn the heat as low as possible. Sprinkle with cinnamon and, having firmly closed the lid, leave to steam for 45 minutes.

Heat the oil and put the *haleem* in a large flat dish. Sprinkle with the almond and pistachio and heated oil. Serve with sugar or honey.

Qoymaq

Sweet spicy dessert

Serves 6   Preparation time: 30 minutes

Qoymaq is noted not only for its nutritional properties but is also prepared as a cure against insomnia.

6 oz (170 g) plain flour
1 pint (550 ml) lukewarm water
1½ pints (850 ml) water
2 tbsp oil *or* knob of butter
50 almonds, chopped
2½ oz (75 g) castor sugar
3 tbsp poppy seeds
1 tbsp ground cardamom

Mix the flour slowly with 1 pint (550 ml) lukewarm water.

Heat 1½ pints (850 ml) water until lukewarm. Mix in the flour paste and bring to boiling point. As soon as the mixture has started to thicken up, add the almonds, poppy seeds and cardamom. Cook until the mixture has turned to jelly, but make sure it does not get too thick.

Serve cold or hot as a sweet dish.

Samanak

Traditional wholemeal pudding

Serves 30

Samanak is a traditional dish prepared to celebrate a fulfilled wish or wishes. The period between the beginning of March and the middle of April is the appropriate season for preparing *samanak* and giving parties. The preparation of *samanak* is preceded by prayer and sing-songs by women.

2 lb (1 kg) whole wheat
11 lb (5 kg) wholemeal flour
3 tbsp poppy seeds
15 whole walnuts

Wash the wheat thoroughly and empty into a muslin cloth or similar fabric which will allow the water to drain away easily. Secure the fabric inside a dish and cover with water. Soak from morning until 8 or 9 in the evening. Drain and place in a strainer to allow water to drain overnight. Soak again for the same length of time. Drain again and place in strainer until morning. Repeat process for third and final time. But remember not to open the cloth during this time.

Untie the cloth on the fourth day, open and check whether germination has started properly. Take either basket or wooden tray(s) and cover the base with muslin or similar fabric. Spread the wheat on it in a layer 1½ inches thick. Place in the light. Sprinkle the wheat and fabric with water twice or even three times daily until the germinating wheat has grown to 1 inch. From then on, water only once in the morning and once at night. Keep the tray slightly tilted so the water does not stagnate. Allow tray to remain in same position until the wheat shoots have grown to 4–4½ inches. This should be maximum length wheat is allowed to grow, because beyond this, the wheat shoots will taste bitter.

Cut the shoots off 1 inch from the wheat seeds. Discard the tops and chop the shoots into small pieces. Put in a food processor and liquidise for some time. Add 1 pint (550 ml) water and extract the juices by squeezing the shoots by hand. Put the residue back into the food processor and run the machine. Again, after adding 1 pint (550 ml) water, extract the juices for a second time. Now keep the first and second extracts to one side in separate dishes. Remember that since the shoots are so strong it is not possible to extract all the juice in one or two operations. Therefore the extracting process should be repeated five or more times. Keep the juice from each operation separately. Discard the residue.

Take a large dish and, keeping aside the first and second grade juice extracts, slowly combine the other extracts with the flour, which should be added little by little, mixing well until the product obtained is slightly thicker than *jelabi* or *pakawra* batter.

How to cook
Take a large, heavy-base non-stick saucepan. Oil it with butter or pure butter ghee. Start on high heat and cook the combined juice. Make sure that you start with a smooth mixture. Stir continuously

until the colour changes to light brown. Add both the first and second juice extracts to it. Keep stirring until the mixture starts to boil and turns brown. Lower the heat level to medium and add hot water every 15 minutes, six times. Add the walnuts and keep boiling until thick bubbles appear. At this stage the *samanak* is ready for steaming. Cover with foil and then with the lid. Steam for 45 minutes on a very low heat.

Serve cold on several dishes after sprinkling with poppy seeds.

Since *samanak* is prepared in large quantities it may not be consumed all at once, but the remainder can be frozen. It is a healthy and non-fattening dish.

Faluda wa jhala

Ice-cream and caramel dessert

Serves 4   *Preparation time: 30 minutes*

2 pints (1 l) milk
½ oz (15 g) agar strip
8 oz (225 g) sugar
1½ tsp ground cardamom
2 tsp (10 ml) rosewater
1 small block vanilla ice-cream
Small amount double cream

Boil the milk, agar and sugar together. Heat until strip has softened. Add the cardamom and rosewater. Mix well for 1 minute and leave aside to cool.

Divide the ice-cream into the required number of helpings. Spoon *zhala* on top, with a small amount of double cream, and serve.

Kishmish paneer

Curd cheese with raisins

Serves 6   Preparation time: 1–2 hours

8 pints (4·5 l) milk
Juice of 2 lemons
Raisins or sultanas

Heat the milk to boiling point. Add the lemon juice
and stir. Remove from the heat.

Place in a clean white cloth and hang over a
basin. Pour cold water on to the cloth to enable
the top to be tied firmly. Leave for 1–2 hours to
cool, and for the water to drain away.

Remove the cloth. Cut the cheese into cubes and
serve with raisins or sultanas.

Semion

Sweet noodles

Serves 6   Preparation time: 30 minutes

1 lb (450 g) wholemeal flour
1 pint (550 ml) water
8 oz (225 g) sugar
1 tsp ground cardamom
5 tbsp (75 ml) oil
½ tsp salt

Gas Mark 6/205°C/400°F

Prepare a firm dough by mixing the flour, sugar and salt with ½ pint (280 ml) water. Use extra water to keep your hands and the dough moist. Add 2 tbsp oil making sure that the dough remains very firm. Leave for 10 minutes.

Shape the dough into several egg-sized balls. Flatten these out so that they are not more than 2 mm thick, and cut into thin lengths. Sprinkle flour liberally over the noodles to stop them sticking together. Leave on a tray to dry out.

Place the noodles in the pre-heated oven until crisp and slightly golden. Remove from the oven and leave to one side.

Boil 3 pints (1·75 l) water. Chop the noodles into approximately 4-inch lengths and add to the boiling water. Cook for 3 more minutes, then drain. Put the noodles back into the saucepan, add

3 tbsp oil with ¼ pint (140 ml) water and mix. Then add another ¼ pint (140 ml) water and sprinkle with cardamom. Wrap the saucepan lid in a clean cloth, cover the pan and steam the noodles for 30 minutes (5 minutes on medium heat and 25 minutes on very low heat).

Serve *semion* hot in a flat dish. Sugar can be added to suit each individual taste.

Halwa-e-zardak

Carrot halva

Serves 6   Preparation time: 1 hour 30 minutes

2 lb (900 g) carrots
4 tbsp (60 ml) corn oil
2 oz (50 g) sugar
2 oz (50 g) almonds
2 oz (50 g) pistachios
½ tbsp cardamom powder
Pinch of saffron
2¼ pints (1·25 l) hot water

Soak the almonds and pistachios in hot water, then peel and cut into pieces.

Wash the carrots, cut the ends off and boil in 1¼ pints (700 ml) water until soft, and then mash.

Heat the oil over a medium flame, add the carrots and fry for 10 minutes until all the water evaporates. Add the sugar, remaining hot water, almonds, pistachios and saffron.

Simmer until the water has evaporated and then leave for 20 minutes on a low heat. Sprinkle with cardamom powder and serve with tea.

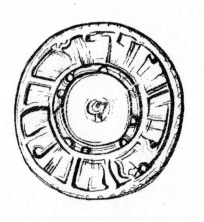

Kulcha Pastries

Gosh-e-feel Elephant-ear pastries

Halwa-e-columba Sweet halva balls

Kulcha-e-birinji Ground rice biscuits

Lojra Sweet crispy pastries

Qutlama Sweet fried pastry

Rout Sweet bread

Kulcha-e-khetay Sweet spicy pastry with semolina

Kulcha qandy Sweet spicy pastry

Cake-e-jawary Corn cake

Kulcha-e-namaki Savoury biscuits

Baqlawa Filo pastry with syrup and nuts

Kulcha-e-nawruzi New Year's pastry

Gosh-e-feel

Elephant-ear pastries

Serves 6   Preparation time: 45 minutes

2 eggs
Pinch salt
¼ pint (140 ml) milk
6 tbsp (90 ml) oil
1 lb (450 g) self-raising flour *or* 1 lb strong white
   flour and ½ tsp bicarbonate of soda
Oil for frying

For the decoration
4 tbsp (60 g) ground pistachio nuts
2 tbsp ground cardamom
8 oz (225 g) icing sugar

Beat the eggs in a large bowl and add the salt and milk.

Sieve the flour and bicarbonate of soda into the egg mixture, blending as you add the flour. Knead well for 5 minutes. Cover with aluminium foil and leave to rest for 15 minutes.

Take a piece of dough the size of a large egg, and roll it out to form a 12-inch circle approximately 1 mm thick. Shape the dough into 'elephant ears' by pleating one side of each dough circle. Wet your fingers to prevent the pleats from drying out and opening.

Heat 1 inch oil in a large frying pan until it is

217

very hot. Fry one *gosh-e-feel* until it changes colour slightly. Turn it and cook the other side. Remove, shake off excess oil and place on kitchen paper to drain.

Sprinkle with the pistachios, cardamon and icing sugar. Leave to cool. Cook each 'elephant ear' in the same way.

Halwa-e-columba

Sweet halva balls

To serve 12   Preparation time: 45 minutes

14 oz (400 g) semolina
7 oz (200 g) sugar
2½ pints (1·25 l) water
4 tbsp (60 ml) water
2 tbsp rosewater
5 pieces round mastic or 3 pieces long mastic
1 lb (450 g) strong white flour
2 tbsp (30 ml) corn oil
Oil for deep-frying

Take 1 tbsp flour and the mastic and grind to a powder in a pestle and mortar. Mix with the semolina and place in a saucepan with the sugar and 2½ pints (1·25 l) water. Slowly bring to the boil, stirring continuously to prevent sticking. Reduce the heat and cook until the water is absorbed and the mixture is thick and creamy (about 2 minutes). Add the rosewater and stir well. Spread the semolina mixture out on a flat plate and leave to cool.

Take the remaining flour and 4 tbsp (60 ml) water. Mix together and knead. Leave to prove for 10 minutes. Measure out 12 tbsp (180 ml) oil. Divide the dough into 6 pieces. Using oil to prevent sticking, roll out each piece of dough until it is tissue-paper thin and about 12 inches square. Coat the dough with oil each time it is rolled. Divide each piece into 6 pieces approximately 6 inches by 4 inches.

Put 1 heaped teaspoonful cooled semolina mixture in the middle of each piece of dough and flatten slightly. Fold the corners over to form a square envelope shape; the edges of the pastry should only just overlap, otherwise the pastry will be too thick and will cook unevenly. Use oil liberally so that the whole parcel sticks together well.

Heat ½ pint (280 ml) oil in a large frying pan and cook the *halwa-e-columba* over a low heat until golden on each side. Remove from the oil, allowing excess to drip back into pan. Sprinkle with castor sugar and ground cardamom. Continue until all the *halwa-e-columba* have been cooked, topping up the oil from time to time.

Serve hot or cold.

Kulcha-e-birinji

Ground rice biscuits

Makes 18   Preparation time: 45 minutes

4 whole eggs
4 egg yolks
½ tsp baking powder
½ lb (225 g) butter
12 oz (340 g) fine rice flour
½ lb (225 g) castor sugar
2 tbsp ground pistachios

Gas Mark 6/205°C/400°F

Break 4 eggs into a medium-sized bowl. Add the egg yolks and baking powder and mix well.

Melt the butter, add to the egg mixture and mix thoroughly. Add the flour and sugar. Mix well and leave to one side.

Grease a baking tray or cut greaseproof paper into rounds the size of a small side plate. Break off a piece of dough, the size of an egg, and flatten it to just smaller than a side plate. Place on the paper or greased baking tray. Using a blunt knife, decorate with vertical and horizontal lines. Bake the biscuits until golden-brown.

Garnish with the ground pistachios and serve with tea.

Lojra

Sweet crispy pastries

Preparation time: 45 minutes

Lojra is an Uzbeki pastry which is eaten with either soup or tea. It is truly an example of the very fine pastry-making talents of the Uzbeki housewife.

A griddle pan is needed for this recipe.

1 lb 8 oz (700 g) strong white flour
1 tbsp salt
¾ pint (425 ml) water
Ghee for coating and frying

Mix all the ingredients together, except the ghee. Divide into 6 pieces and leave to prove for 10 minutes.

Roll out each piece to about 14 inches square. Brush all over with ghee and roll each one up. Cut each into 2 or 3 pieces.

Take 1 piece of rolled dough at a time and cut into 12 or 18 pieces. Roll each piece roughly into a large cigar shape. Then twist it to form a spiral shape. Press the ends together to make a circle and then expand the ring with your fingers until it is approximately 4 inches or 6 inches in diameter, depending on whether you cut the original large piece of dough into 2 or 3 pieces.

Heat the griddle pan. Cook the dough pieces on low heat until they are golden on each side.

Lojra will keep for up to 2 weeks in a refrigerator.

Qutlama

Sweet fried pastry

Serves 12   Preparation time: 45 minutes

Qutlama is eaten hot or cold. It can be eaten at any meal, on picnics or with tea. *Qutlama* is also served at weddings.

2 lb (900 g) strong white flour
1 tbsp salt
1 pint (550 ml) water
1 lb 6 oz (625 g) soft margarine
Vegetable oil
Castor sugar and finely chopped pistachios to
  garnish

Stir the water and salt very gradually into the flour and knead into a firm dough. Divide into 5 equal portions and knead each thoroughly. Cover with foil and leave to prove for 10–15 minutes.

Knead each portion well and work into a ball. Taking 1 ball at time, roll out to approximately 16 inches square. Spread half of the square with melted margarine, using pastry brush or fingers. Fold the dough over. Repeat this procedure twice more, spreading completely with melted margarine. Fold over the ends to seal in the margarine and carefully press down. Using your hands and turning the dough often, gently stretch it to the size of a side plate (about 7 inches in diameter).

223

There are many forms of decoration, but here is one which is popular and simple. Prick the dough underneath with a fork and then, using the blunt side of a knife, mark it with parallel straight lines on the top. Half turn the dough and make crossing lines. Take a cup and impress 5 overlapping circles on the dough.

Take a frying pan approximately 10 inches in diameter. Add 12 tbsp (180 ml) oil. Slowly fry the pastry, making holes in it with the blunt end of a fork to allow the oil to come through. Cook until golden (about 5 minutes). Turn the pastry over and continue to cook over a low heat. When it is golden underneath, remove from the oil, drain, then place on kitchen paper.

Sprinkle with castor sugar and finely chopped pistachios.

Rout

Sweet bread

Serves 8   Preparation time: 45 minutes

1 lb (450 g) castor sugar
4 eggs
½ tsp baking powder
½ tbsp fresh yeast
3 lb (1·5 kg) plain flour
1 tbsp ground cardamom
3 tbsp rosewater
½ lb (225 g) margarine, melted
1 pint (550 ml) milk
1 small carton sour cream
1 tbsp cous cous
1 tbsp sesame seeds
1 tbsp onion seeds

Gas mark 5/190°C/370°F then Gas Mark
   7/220°C/430°F

Take a medium-sized bowl and mix together the
sugar, eggs, yeast, baking powder, flour, cardamom and rosewater. Add the melted margarine
and rub well with fingertips. Add the milk and
sour cream and mix together thoroughly. Put a
clean cloth on top of the bowl and leave for 1 hour
in a warm place to prove.
   Pre-heat the oven to Gas Mark 5.
   Divide the dough into 8 balls. Roll each one

out into a circle ½ inch thick. Put on pieces of greaseproof paper, slightly larger than the dough circles.

Prick the top of the dough all over with a fork in vertical and horizontal lines. Sprinkle with cous cous, sesame seeds and onion seeds.

Bake in the oven for 15 minutes then increase the heat to Gas Mark 7. When the bread is light golden-brown, remove from the oven and leave to cool.

Serve with tea.

Kulcha-e-khetay

Sweet spicy pastry with semolina

Makes 15   Preparation time: 1 hour

5 oz (135 g) self-raising flour
5 oz (135 g) chickpea flour
5 oz (135 g) semolina
½ lb (225 g) castor sugar
12 tbsp (180 ml) pure ghee
3 tbsp chopped pistachios
1 tbsp ground cardamom

Gas Mark 6/205°C/400°F

Mix the flours with the oil and ground cardamom. Add the castor sugar and knead well. Leave for 30 minutes to rest.

Preheat the oven.

Divide the dough into 15 balls and flatten into 1-inch rounds. Press your thumb into the middle, turning your thumb nearly a full circle. Place some pistachio in the central hollow. Arrange the pastries on a greased baking tray and bake for 10–15 minutes. Check every now and then that the pastries are browning before taking them out of the oven.

Kulcha-e-qandy

Sweet spicy pastry

Makes 30   Preparation time: 1 hour

2 lb (1 kg) plain flour
1 lb (450 g) butter
1 lb (450 g) icing sugar
½ tbsp ground cardamom
3 tbsp finely chopped pistachio nuts

Gas Mark 7/220°C/430°F

Mix the flour and butter very well. Add the sugar, pistachio nuts and cardamom and leave for 15 minutes. Cut the dough into several egg-sized pieces. Flatten each piece into 3-inch rounds. Place on a well-greased baking tray or put each pastry separately on greased paper.

Cook in the pre-heated oven for 10–15 minutes until golden-brown.

Cake-e-jawary

Corn cake

Serves 6   Preparation time: 30 minutes

Pinch saffron
10 oz (280 g) cornflour
8 oz (225 g) icing sugar
2 cups (360 ml) corn oil
1 small carton natural yoghurt
2 tsp rosewater
½ tsp baking powder
9 oz (250 g) blanched almonds
1 tsp cardamom powder
4 large eggs
1 lb (450 g) coarse semolina

For the icing
1½ lb (700 g) icing sugar
1 pint (550 ml) water

Gas Mark 6/205°C/400°F

To make the icing, boil the water and sugar until syrupy and slightly thick. Keep to one side. Mix all the cake ingredients except the almonds.

Lightly grease a medium-sized tin. Add the mixture and level out. Arrange the almonds in rows on top, leaving enough space to cut between them.

Preheat the oven. Bake the cake for 10–15 minutes until the top is golden-brown. Turn the oven off and leave the cake for 5 more minutes in the oven.

Take the cake out of the oven and cut into squares. Allow to cool in the tin and then pour on the icing. Allow to set before removing from the tin.

Kulcha-e-namaki

Savoury biscuits

Serves 12   Preparation time: 1 hour 45 minutes

1 lb 4 oz (625 g) plain flour
8 oz (225 g) butter
2 eggs
½ tbsp yeast
3 tbsp sour cream
½ tbsp salt
5 tbsp milk
1 tbsp onion seeds

Gas Mark 6/205°C/400°F

Mix flour, egg, yeast, sour cream, butter and salt thoroughly and add the milk. Knead the dough and leave to one side for 1 hour.

Shape the dough into 15 balls just larger than ping-pong balls. Prick the sides of each one lightly with a knife. Then press down on the tops with your fist. Sprinkle with onion seeds and cook in the pre-heated oven for 15 minutes, until golden-brown.

Serve with tea.

Baqlawa

Filo pastry with syrup and nuts

Serves 12   Preparation time: 45 minutes

You may buy ready-made filo pastry instead of making your own.

For the syrup
12 oz (340 g) sugar
1 pint (550 ml) water

For the pastry
15 oz (425 g) strong white flour
1 egg
6 tbsp (90 ml) oil
¼ pint (140 ml) milk
1 tsp dried yeast
½ tsp bicarbonate of soda

For the filling
1 lb (450 g) walnuts, ground finely
3 oz (85 g) almonds, ground finely
Butter
Ground cardamom to garnish

Gas Mark 6/205°C/400°F

Make a syrup by boiling the sugar and water.
   Place 8 oz (225 g) flour in a bowl. Blend the yeast with a little milk and add to the flour with the oil. Blend the bicarbonate of soda with a little milk and add. Rub in well. Add the remaining milk and

232

knead well. Break the egg into the middle of the dough and knead thoroughly. Cover with a damp cloth and leave for 5 minutes.

Divide the dough into 10 pieces and roll out as thin as tissue paper, approximately 10 by 13 inches. Use the remaining flour to keep the board well covered.

Take 1 leaf of pastry. Rub the surface with butter and sprinkle with a little ground walnut and ground almond. Repeat with all the pastry leaves, buttering both sides of the pastry.

Butter a baking dish approximately 10 by 13 inches. Fill with the pastry. Cut into triangular shapes and bake until golden-brown (about 15 minutes).

Remove the *baqlawa* from the oven and pour the syrup over so that it soaks right through to the bottom layer. Allow time for the syrup to be absorbed. Garnish with the ground cardamom and the rest of the walnut and almond. Leave to cool.

Kulcha-e-nawruzi

New Year's pastry

Serves 12   Preparation time: 30 minutes

2 lb 4 oz (1 kg) rice flour/ground rice
1 lb 2 oz (500 g) butter
1 lb 5 oz (600 g) icing sugar
4 egg whites
4 eggs
½ tsp baking powder
1 tsp ground cardamom
3 tbsp rosewater
2 tbsp ground pistachios

Gas Mark 6/205°C/400°F

Cream the butter in a bowl. Add the egg white and egg and mix until firm. You may not need to use all the butter. Add the baking powder, flour, sugar, cardamom and rosewater. Mix and leave aside for 4 hours.

Divide the dough into several egg-size balls. Flatten each ball to the size of a small saucer and decorate with the tip of a knife or spoon.

Sprinkle pistachio powder over the pastries and arrange them on a flat oven dish. Bake in the pre-heated oven for 15 minutes. Remove from the oven while still yellowish in colour.

Muraba Jams

Muraba-e-alobolow Cherry jam

Muraba-e-behy Pawpaw jam

Muraba-e-zardak Carrot jam with nuts

Muraba-e-khilal-e-norange Orange and nut jam

Muraba-e-zanjabeel Ginger jam

Muraba

The warm climate in Afghanistan produces a great variety of the finest fruits. We eat a lot of fruit, serving it also at the end of a meal. Each household takes great pride in making its own jam which we eat for breakfast and afternoon tea. We also serve it as an accompaniment to some *pelau, chalau,* and *shola* dishes, for example *Yakhni pelau* (p. 150).

Muraba-e-alobolow

Cherry jam

2 lb (900 g) cooking cherries
¾ lb (340 g) castor sugar
½ pint (280 ml) water
Juice of 1 small lemon

Wash the cherries thoroughly and remove the stones without damaging the fruit.

Mix the cherries and sugar and leave aside for approximately 20 minutes, after which time the juice from the cherries should start to flow. Add the water and lemon juice and warm gently so that the sugar dissolves.

Bring to the boil, cooking rapidly until the juice reaches a thick, syrupy consistency.

Take the saucepan off the heat and leave to one side for 24 hours.

Bottle in sterilised jars and store in a cool place, where the jam will keep indefinitely.

Muraba-e-behy

Pawpaw jam

2 lb (900 g) pawpaws
1½ lb (700 g) sugar
1 tsp cardamom powder
4 tbsp lemon juice
2 pints (1 l) water
½ tsp saffron

Skin the pawpaws, remove the seeds and cut into ½-inch cubes. Put into a heavy saucepan with the water. Bring slowly to the boil and simmer until the pawpaw is soft (approximately 10 minutes).

Add the sugar and boil at medium temperature until the liquid is syrupy.

Add the cardamom, lemon juice and saffron and continue to cook on a low heat for another 10 minutes.

Leave to cool. Bottle in sterilised jars.

Muraba-e-behy can also be used as a dessert with double cream, or as an accompaniment to *chalau* rice (p. 135).

Muraba-e-zardak

Carrot jam with nuts

2 lb (900 g) carrots
¼ tsp saffron
1 lb (450 g) sugar
2¾ pints (1·5 l) water
3½ oz (100 g) pistachios soaked in hot water,
  peeled and cut into 2
3½ oz (100 g) almonds soaked in hot water,
  peeled and cut into 4
30 whole green cardamoms
Juice of 2 lemons

Wash the carrots, slice thinly and cut into long strips.

Dissolve the saffron in ¼ pint (140 ml) water.

Dissolve the sugar with the rest of the water and boil for 5 minutes, then add the carrots, pistachios, almonds, cardamoms and lemon juice and boil for 15 minutes until the carrots are slightly soft. Add the saffron and leave to cool.

Put in an airtight jar and store in a cool place. The jam may be kept for several months.

Serve at tea time.

Muraba-e-khilal-e-norange

Orange jam with nuts

10 oranges
1 lb (450 g) sugar
Pinch of saffron, dissolved in ¼ pint (140 ml)
  water
3½ oz (100 g) pistachios, soaked in hot water,
  peeled and cut into 2
3½ oz (100 g) almonds, soaked in hot water,
  peeled and cut into 4
20 whole green cardamoms
Juice of 2 lemons

Slice off the stalk ends of the oranges and cut them
vertically into quarters. Peel off the skin, discard
the pith and the flesh, and cut the peel into long,
strips. Cover with water and bring to the boil for
5 minutes and drain. Repeat until the skin is tender
but not too soft.

Dissolve the sugar in 1 pint (550 ml) water and
boil for 10 minutes until syrupy. Add the saffron,
pistachios, almonds, cardamoms, lemon juice and
orange peel. Boil for 3 minutes. If too thick, add
¼ pint (140 ml) hot water. Leave to cool and store
in a jar.

Muraba-e-zanjabeel

Ginger jam

1 lb (450 g) fresh ginger
1 pint (550 ml) water
¼ lb (110 g) sugar
2 tsp vinegar
Juice of 2 lemons
Pinch of saffron

Peel the ginger and cut into ½-inch cubes.

Boil the water and add the ginger and vinegar.
Boil for 20 minutes.

Add the sugar and lemon juice and boil for 10
minutes. Add the saffron and leave to cool.

Pour into a sterilised jar. This jam can be kept
for up to a year.

Turshi-e-chutni Pickles and chutnies

Turshi badrang Cucumber pickle

Turshi poste limo Lemon pickle

Chutni morch-e-sorkhe Chilli chutney

Chutni gashneez Coriander chutney

Chutni sabz Green chutney

Chutni morch sabz Green pepper chutney

Morch masaladar Chilli powder condiment

Uzbeki chutni Uzbeki chutney for chalau dishes

Turshi badrang

Cucumber pickle

1 pint (550 ml) white vinegar or 1½ pints (750 ml)
  lemon juice
½ pint (280 ml) water
4 tsp salt
2 tbsp sugar
2 lb (900 g) cucumber
2 to 3 sprigs fresh coriander, cut into 1-inch pieces

Mix the vinegar or lemon juice and the water and
bring to the boil. Add 2 tsp salt and sugar. Stir
until the salt and sugar are dissolved. Cool.

Wash and dry the cucumbers. Slice lengthways
into quarters, and then into roughly 3-inch lengths.

Put the cucumber into a colander and mix with
the remaining salt. Place the colander in the sink.
Put a plate over cucumbers and a weight on top of
the plate. Leave until the water has drained from
the cucumbers – approximately 30 minutes.

Fill a sterilised jar with cucumbers to within 1
inch of the top. Cover with vinegar or lemon juice,
add the fresh coriander and seal.

Keep the jar in a dry, cool place for 1 week before
using.

Turshi poste limo

Lemon pickle

2 lb (900 g) lemons
2 tsp salt
½ tsp sugar
1 pint (550 ml) white vinegar
¼ pint (140 ml) water

Cut the lemons in half and extract the juice.
Remove the pith and fleshy part, leaving the peel.
Place the peel in cold water for 3 days. Drain.

Bring the peel to the boil in fresh cold water.
Add the salt and sugar. Boil for 10 minutes. Drain.

Bring skins to the boil in the vinegar and ¼ pint
(140 ml) water. Boil for 10 minutes and then allow
to cool.

Fill a sterilised jar with the lemon peel to within
1 inch of the top. Cover with the vinegar and water
mixture and seal.

Store in a cool, dry place. After 1 week the pickle
will be ready to serve.

Chutni morch-e-sorkhe

Chilli chutney

½ lb (225 g) fresh red chillies
1 pint (550 g) white vinegar
¼ pint (140 ml) water
½ tsp sugar
¼ tsp salt
5 cloves garlic, finely crushed
A few mint leaves

Remove the stalk and seeds from the chillies.
   Mix the vinegar and water. Bring to the boil for
5 minutes. Add the sugar, salt and crushed garlic.
   Pack the chillies in a sterilised jar. Cover the
chillies with liquid and add the mint leaves.
   Seal the jar and leave for 15 days before using.

Chutni gashneez

Coriander chutney

3 bunches fresh coriander
2 large cloves garlic
½ lb (225 g) walnuts
¼ lb (110 g) blanched almonds
2 oz (50 g) green chillies
1 tsp salt
1 tsp black pepper
1 tsp white vinegar *or* lemon juice

Mix all the ingredients except the vinegar in an electric blender. Add the white vinegar or lemon juice to obtain a runny consistency.

Bottle and keep for 2 days before use.

Chutni sabz

Green chutney

This chutney comes from North Afghanistan, where vegetables and grapes are grown. It is always made very hot, but the amount of green chillies can be reduced according to taste. This one is medium-hot for average taste.

3 large green chillies
7 oz (200 g) green grapes
2 large cloves garlic
½ tsp salt
¼ pint (140 ml) plain yoghurt

De-seed the green chillies and the grapes. Finely chop in an electic blender, adding the salt and garlic. Stir in the yoghurt.
    Serve fresh.

Chutni morch sabz

Green pepper chutney

8 oz (225 g) green peppers
2 oz (50 g) walnuts *or* almonds
4 cloves garlic
2 oz (50 g) dried coriander
2 tsp sugar
1 pint (550 ml) white vinegar
1 tsp olive oil

Cut the peppers in half and remove the seeds. Leave peppers to one side in cold water.

Finely chop the walnuts (or almonds) and garlic.

Remove the peppers from the water and dry them. Finely chop the peppers and coriander in a food processor.

Mix the sugar with 6 tsp water and bring slowly to the boil. Add the vinegar and ¼ pint (140 ml) water. Boil for 5 minutes. Leave to cool and then stir in 1 tsp olive oil.

Bottle and use after 2 days.

Morch masaladar

Chilli powder condiment

1 lb (450 g) dried chillies
2 oz (50 g) walnuts
2 oz (50 g) dried coriander
10 whole cardamoms
½ tsp garlic powder
½ tsp salt

Wash the chillies and remove stalks. Grind to a powder in an electric grinder. Put aside.

Grind the walnuts in the same way. Grind the dried coriander. Grind the whole cardamoms.

Mix all the ingredients together. Store in a jar out of reach of children.

Uzbeki chutni

Uzbeki chutney for chalau dishes

4 onions
2 tsp salt
1 tsp sugar
2 tsp hot chilli powder
3 tomatoes
3 tsp vinegar

Peel and cut the onions into thin slices. Rub the salt, sugar and chilli powder into the onions with your fingers.

Blend the tomatoes in a liquidiser. Add the remaining ingredients and mix well.

Serve with *chalau* rice (p. 135).

Chai Tea and beverages

Chai-e-sia Black tea

Chai-e-shibet Dill tea

Chai-e-sabz Green tea

Chai-e-chawa Ginger tea with walnuts

Kaymak chai Green tea with clotted cream

Kaymak chai Green tea, English style

Dogh Yoghurt drink with mint and cucumber

Chai

We drink a lot of tea in Afghanistan, but we do not drink coffee except on very rare occasions. There is always someone drinking tea at home, especially after work, as we believe it helps to combat fatigue.

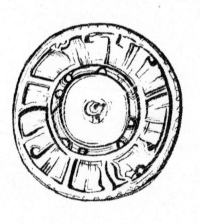

Chai-e-sia

Black tea

Serves 3

1 tsp black tea
1 pint (550 ml) water
1 tsp cardamom powder
1 lemon
Pinch of saffron

Wash the tea with boiling water. Stir it well. Pour off the water. This process removes any dust and colouring.

Put the tea into a warmed teapot with a pinch of saffron and up to 1 pint (550 ml) boiling water, depending on how many people you are serving. Add 1 tsp cardamom powder.

The tea can be served after 3 minutes, with fresh lemon.

Chai-e-shibet

Dill tea

Serves 3

Dill tea is drunk in Afghanistan because we believe that it is very effective in cleansing the kidneys, controlling blood pressure and eliminating cholesterol.

1 pint (550 ml) water
1 tsp dill
5 whole cardamoms, with skins split
¼ tsp dried mint *or* 1 tsp fresh grated ginger
Juice of ½ lemon

Put the dill, cardamom and mint (or ginger) in a stainless-steel teapot. Add the boiling water. Leave for 5 minutes to draw. Pour and add lemon juice.

Chai-e-sabz

Green tea

Serves 6

1½ tsp green tea
5 whole cardamoms, with skins split
1 pint (550 ml) water

Put the green tea and the cardamoms in a stainless-steel teapot. Pour on the boiling water.

Put on lowest heat possible for 1 minute and then serve.

Chai-e-chawa

Ginger tea with walnuts

Serves 4

Chawa tea is traditionally recommended for people suffering from rheumatism.

4 oz (110 g) fresh ginger, crushed
½ tsp dried ginger
4 oz (110 g) sugar
1 tsp ground cardamom
7 walnuts, finely chopped
1 pint (550 ml) water

Chop the fresh ginger and walnuts finely. Boil the water and pour into stainless-steel teapot. Add all the ingredients and boil for 2 more minutes. Leave to draw for 2 minutes and serve.

Kaymak chai

Green tea with clotted cream

For the kaymak (clotted cream)

4 pints (2·25 l) milk
1 small carton double cream
2 tbsp plain flour

In a medium saucepan, heat the milk and double cream to boiling point. Lower heat. Fill a ladle and pour the contents back into the saucepan from as high as possible. Repeat this another 4 times until bubbles appear.

Sieve the flour into the milk and cream mixture. As the mixture thickens, remove the top and put it in a bowl. Cook and remove the *kaymak* as it forms, until a small amount of milk remains. Return the *kaymak* to the stove and continue to cook over the lowest heat possible for 3 to 4 hours.

For the chai
3 pints (1·75 l) water
2 tbsp green tea
1 lb (450 g) sugar
2 tbsp ground cardamom
1 tsp baking powder
½ pint (280 ml) cold water or ice cubes
4 pints (2·25 l) milk

Bring the tea and water to the boil in a saucepan until tea leaves have expanded. Boil for 10 minutes. Add the baking powder. Boil for a further few minutes and strain. The tea will rise to the top of the saucepan during boiling. Each time it does, put in an ice cube to reduce the temperature.

Put 2 tbsp cold water into another saucepan. Pour the tea into the second saucepan. Put another 2 tbsp cold water into the original saucepan and pour the tea back into it. Repeat this procedure 5 times so that the tea will have been poured 5 times from each saucepan.

Add the milk. Bring to the boil. The colour of the tea should be light pink. Add the sugar and cardamom.

Pour the tea into cups and put 1 tbsp *kaymak* on the top.

Kebab-e-dosh (p. 104) and *naun-e-roghani* (p. 5) are usually eaten with *kaymak chai*.

Kaymak chai

Green tea, English style

1 pint (550 ml) milk
4 tsp Ceylon tea
5 cloves
5 cardamoms, with outer skin split
Ground cardamom
Clotted cream

Boil the milk. Add the tea, cardamom and cloves. Simmer until the tea turns dark pink and add ¼ pint (140 ml) water. Pour into a teapot.

To serve, pour the tea into the teacups. Slide 2 tsp clotted cream on top. Sprinkle with ground cardamom.

Dogh

Yoghurt drink with mint and cucumber

2 lb (1 kg) low-fat natural yoghurt
¼ tsp salt
½ tsp dried mint
¼ large cucumber *or* 1 small cucumber
10 ice cubes

Blend all the ingredients except cucumber for 5 minutes in a food processor. Add the very finely chopped cucumber and chill. If it is too thick to drink, add water.

Dogh will keep in a refrigerator for up to 2 days.

Index

Index

Index

267

Index

271

Index

Index

273

Index

274